14

THE
Archive Photographs
SERIES

P&A CAMPBELL
PLEASURE STEAMERS
1887-1945

The flagship of the White Funnel Fleet from 1896 to 1946, the *Britannia*, steams up the River Avon under the Clifton Suspension Bridge, on Bank Holiday Monday 1 August 1938.

THE
Archive Photographs
SERIES

P&A CAMPBELL
PLEASURE STEAMERS
1887-1945

Compiled by
Chris Collard

TEMPUS

First published 1999
Copyright © Chris Collard, 1999

Tempus Publishing Limited
The Mill, Brimscombe Port,
Stroud, Gloucestershire, GL5 2QG

ISBN 0 7524 1711 8

Typesetting and origination by
Tempus Publishing Limited
Printed in Great Britain by
Midway Clark Printing, Wiltshire

Acknowledgements

The photographs contained in this book are taken from my collection, which has been assembled during the course of the past forty years from a wide variety of sources. It is impossible to acknowledge the origin of each illustration, but I wish to record my sincere gratitude to the following individuals and institutions: Mr Nigel Coombes, Mr Lionel Vaughan, the late H.A. Allen, the late Ernest Dumbleton, the late Edwin Keen, the Bristol Records Office and Mrs Joy Slocombe of the Ilfracombe Museum. My particular thanks are extended to Mr George Owen, the leading authority on the Bristol Channel steamers, not only for permission to reproduce many of his own excellent photographs, but also for his meticulous checking of my manuscript.

Contents

BRISTOL CHANNEL SERVICES

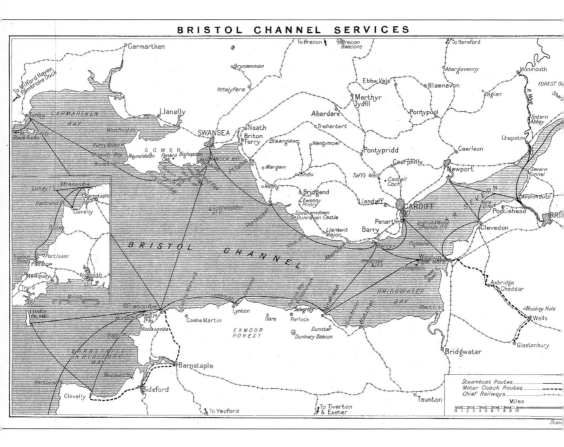

SOUTH COAST SERVICES

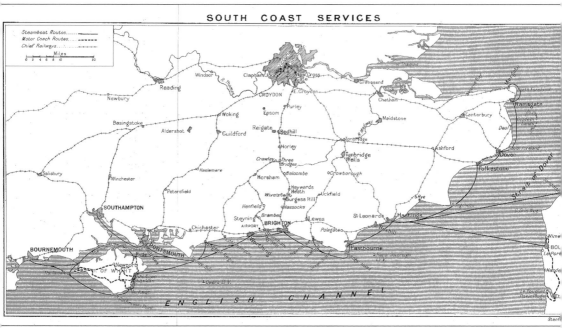

Introduction

The paddle steamers of the White Funnel Fleet of P&A Campbell Ltd plied the waters of the Bristol Channel and the South Coast for over seventy years. They became so much a part of people's lives that hardly a day at the seaside passed without a sight of at least one.

In the depths of winter the ships lay forlorn and deserted in the Bristol City Docks, but with the approach of spring they came to life as the shipyard workers prepared them for another season. They were the harbingers of summers which never seemed to end and days when the sun always shone.

In reality, history tells a somewhat different story and the company had to contend with the financial constraints of many summers of appalling weather. Difficulties of a more serious nature were faced and overcome; even two World Wars and the intervening years of the Depression could not daunt the spirit of enterprise and determination which characterised all of the company's endeavours.

The seaside resorts of Great Britain had become firmly established during the latter half of the twentieth century. An increasing awareness of the benefits of sea air beckoned the population to the coast, and the growing public demand to be taken to and from the holiday resorts led to the development of marine excursions.

Since the early 1800s various ports on the Bristol Channel had been linked by the services of the packet steamers – vessels which ran on regular passenger-carrying routes in both summer and winter – but the day excursions, as we now know them, did not begin until the late 1880s. During the summer of 1887 the paddle steamer *Waverley*, owned by the Campbell family of Kilmun, Dumbartonshire, ran day trips in the Bristol Channel, on charter to a syndicate of Bristolians.

The Campbells had been shipowners since the mid-nineteenth century, operating passenger services on the Firth of Clyde, but in the 1880s, in common with similar small companies, they were facing the prospect of considerable competition from the Caledonian Steam Packet Co., a subsidiary of the Caledonian Railway. This company was branching out into the shipowning business, with plans for a large fleet of superior vessels. The Campbells could see that such a development heralded the demise of the smaller companies. They therefore sought a new area of operations. Following the successful completion of the *Waverley*'s 1887 charter, the Campbell brothers, Peter and Alexander, considered the Bristol Channel to be an area ripe for the development of marine excursions.

The *Waverley* returned to Bristol in 1888 with Capt. Alec in command, running her on his own account, while Capt. Peter remained in Scotland supervising the operation of their two other steamers, *Madge Wildfire* and *Meg Merrilies*. Although the *Waverley*'s 1888 season was not a great financial success, the brothers were convinced that their future lay in the estuary of the River Severn. The actual transfer of business took effect from 1 January 1889, the same date on which, in a very shrewd move, the brothers sold the *Madge* and the *Meg* to the Caledonian Steam Packet Co.

With their move to Bristol, the brothers faced several daunting problems. Not least were the hazards of the channel itself, the rise and fall of its tide being among the largest in the world. Rapid tidal flow, swirling currents in the rock-studded channels and numerous mud- and sandbanks posed navigational problems, while the fact that many of its landing places and their approaches dried out at low tide called for precise planning with regard to the scheduling of timetables. Furthermore, unlike the sheltered waters of the Firth of Clyde, the lower reaches of the channel were exposed to the full fury of the Atlantic gales.

In addition, the brothers met with intense rivalry and competition from other local steamship operators, but they were ideally suited to face the task which they had undertaken. Both Peter and Alec were skilled navigators and ship handlers. In stature and character, however, they were quite different. Peter was a big, robust man with a personality and sense of humour to match. He possessed considerable engineering skills and was one of the few men of the period who obtained both a Master's and an Engineer's certificate. Alec, on the other hand, was a short, slight man with a quiet and genial nature who possessed exceptional business acumen. They were, in fact, an ideal combination and ran their company with great efficiency, rapidly earning the overwhelming respect and friendship of their passengers.

P&A Campbell became a limited company in 1893 and by the end of the century their fleet had increased from one ship to ten. They had extended their services to the South Coast and had established themselves as one of the major operators of pleasure steamers in the country.

The heyday of the paddle steamer ended with the outbreak of the First World War in August 1914, but even then, their pioneering continued when two White Funnel steamers were taken over by the Admiralty for trials as minesweepers. These vessels proved eminently suited to the task and paved the way for the requisitioning of most of the country's paddle steamers for similar duties.

At the end of the hostilities the surviving vessels returned to their peacetime duties only to face years of industrial unrest and depression. Nevertheless, with careful management and planning, the company's comprehensive network of services more than satisfied the demands of the travelling public.

With the outbreak of the Second World War, all of the White Funnel steamers were again requisitioned by the Admiralty. This time the toll of losses was greater and only four of the paddle steamers returned to civilian service. What lay ahead for P&A Campbell could only be conjectured, but the dark years of war were over; the popularity of the boat trip endured and a spirit of optimism prevailed.

One

The Bristol Channel before the First World War

Left: Captain Peter Campbell (1858-1938). *Right:* Captain Alec Campbell (1862-1928).

Ilfracombe, *c*.1869. Before day excursions became a regular feature in the Bristol Channel, a number of packet steamers catered, in a small way, for the day trippers. This view, which pre-dates the building of Ilfracombe pier, shows the Swansea to Bristol packet *Velindra* (left) embarking passengers from Wharf House Point. Centre is the *Éclair*, which ran between Portishead and Ilfracombe three times weekly going down-channel one day and back the next. On the right is an unidentified paddle tug – possibly the *Star* of Cardiff.

Ilfracombe, 1887. Construction of the pier began in 1870 and was completed in 1873 under the auspices of the Lord of the Manor, Sir Bourchier Palk Wrey. The fourteenth-century Chapel of St Nicholas, Patron Saint of Sailors, overlooked the pier from the top of Lantern Hill. The chapel was once a dwelling house inhabited by a husband and wife and their fourteen children! The *Waverley* (right), the first White Funnel steamer to sail in the Bristol Channel, lies at the face of the pier while on the left, at the Stone Bench, is the *Rio Formoso*, owned by Pockett's of Swansea. She was principally a cargo steamer but was certified to carry a small number of passengers.

Ilfracombe and Bristol.

The Bristol General Steam Navigation Company's

FAST   SAILING

STEAM   VESSEL

TORRIDGE,

CAPTAIN WILLIAM PARFITT,

is intended to sail as follows during the Month of SEPTEMBER 1849.

The only Steamer going direct, and that lands and embarks Passengers at the Pier without the aid of Boats.

BRISTOL to ILFRACOMBE.							ILFRACOMBE to BRISTOL.						
Saturday,	Sept.	1,	..	..	5½	Morning	Monday,	Sept.	3,	..	..	3	Morning
Wednesday,	,,	5,	..	..	7½	Morning	Thursday,	,,	6,	..	..	9	Morning
Saturday,	,,	8,	..	..	9	Morning	Monday,	,,	10,	..	..	12	Noon
Wednesday,	,,	12,	..	..	1½	Afternoon	Thursday,	,,	13,	..	..	4	Morning
Saturday,	,,	15,	..	..	5	Morning	Monday,	,,	17,	..	..	8	Morning
Wednesday,	,,	19,	..	..	7½	Morning	Thursday,	,,	20,	..	..	9	Morning
Saturday,	,,	22,	..	..	9	Morning	Monday,	,,	24,	..	..	11	Morning
Wednesday,	,,	26,	..	..	12	Noon	Thursday,	,,	27,	..	..	3	Morning
Saturday,	,,	29,	..	..	4	Morning	Monday,	Oct.	1,	..	..	7	Morning

LYNMOUTH & LYNTON.—The Torridge calls off Lynmouth, going to and returning from Ilfracombe, weather permitting. Passengers landed and embarked on payment of 1s. each. Luggage to be paid for at a moderate charge, for which purpose a large boat is always in attendance. For particulars, apply to Mr. Thos. Baker, Lynton.

FARES:—Cabin, 11s., Children, under 12 years of age, 6s.; Servants, 8s., including Steward's Fee.; Deck, 5s.; Children, under 12 years of age, 2s. 6d.; Carriage, 50s.; Pair-Horse Phæton 40s.; Small One-Horse Phæton, 30s.; Gig, 21s.; Horse, 21s.; Dog, 2s. 6d.

☞ Particulars obtained at the Bristol General Steam Navigation Company's Office, Quay, Bristol; Mr. Martin, Ilfracombe; Mr. R. Stacey, Carmarthen; Mr. J. N. Smart, Swansea; and Mr T. Baker, Lynton.

NOTICE.—The Proprietors of the above Steam-Packet will not be accountable for any Cabin Passenger's Luggage (if lost or damaged) above the value of £5; nor for any Deck Passenger's Luggage (if lost or damaged) above the value of 20s.; unless in each case entered as such, and freight in proportion paid for the same at the time of delivery; nor will they be answerable for any other parcel above the value of 40s. (if lost or damaged), unless entered as such and freight in proportion paid for the same at the time of delivery.

Not accountable for any Goods without Shipping Notes.

☞ *All Letters seeking information to be post-paid.*

Bristol, September, 1849.

Philip Rose, Printer, at the (late) Mechanics' Institution, Broadmead, Bristol.

A timetable for one of the packet steamers running between Bristol and Ilfracombe. It presents a wealth of fascinating information, including the fares for servants as well as horses and carriages.

CHARTER PARTY.

2, RUMFORD PLACE,

LIVERPOOL, *April 27* 188*7*

It is this day mutually agreed between *Alexander Campbell Glasgow* Owner ~~or Captain duly authorized by the owner~~ of the good *Paddle* Steam Ship, called the *Waverley* of *244* Tons gross Register, and *33* Tons nett Register, *99* horses' power

and *C. H. Tucker of Bristol* Merchants and Charterers.

WITNESSETH,

That the said *A. Campbell Esq* agree to let, and the said *C. H. Tucker* agree to hire the said Steam Ship for the term of *Five* calendar Months, from ~~the~~ *October the 18th* day of *May next* she being then placed at the disposal of the Charterers at *Glasgow* in such Dock, or at such safe Wharf or place (where she may always safely lie afloat), as Charterers may direct, she being then tight, staunch, and strong, and every way fitted for the service ~~(and with full complement of officers, seamen, engineers, and firemen (as a vessel of her tonnage)~~; to be employed in such lawful trades, between ports in the ~~United Kingdom, or on the Continent~~ *Bristol Channel within the limits of her passenger Certificates to be used as a Passenger Steamer The Steamer to be fitted with a Surface Condenser*

~~as Charterers or their Agents shall direct, on the following conditions :—~~

That the Owners shall provide ~~and pay for all the provisions and pay of the Captain, Officers, Engineers, Firemen, and Crew~~ *Hull only*; shall pay for the Insurance on the Vessel; also, for all engine-room stores, and maintain her in a thoroughly efficient state in hull and machinery for the service. That the Charterers shall provide and pay for all the *Crew* Coals, Fuel, Port Charges, Pilotages, Agencies, Commissions, and all other charges whatsoever, except those before stated.

That the Charterers shall pay for the use and hire of the said vessel at the rate of *Three Hundred Fifty Pounds* per ~~gross register Ton~~ *£350* per calendar Month, commencing on the day of *delivery* instant, at and after the same rates for any part of a Month; hire to continue from the time specified for terminating the Charter, until her delivery to Owners (unless lost) at *Glasgow*

Payment to be made in Cash

in advance monthly

and in default of such payment or payments as herein specified, the Owners shall have the faculty of withdrawing the said Steamer from the service of the Charterers, without prejudice to any claim they, the Owners, may have on the Charterers, in pursuance of this Charter *The Steamer to be the d*

~~This Demurrage or cargo, shall be laden and discharged in any dock, or at any wharf or place that Charterers may direct, where she can always safely lie afloat.~~

A copy of the Charter Party document for the *Waverley*'s season at Bristol in 1887.

The *Waverley* in the Avon Gorge, 1887. The *Waverley* had been built in 1885 for the Campbells' Glasgow to Kilmun route but was found to be somewhat too large for that service. The offer of a charter for the summer of 1887 from a Bristol syndicate – The Bristol Channel Marine Excursion Co. – was eagerly accepted.

The *Lady Margaret* (1) at Cardiff. Edwards, Robertson & Co. of Cardiff entered the excursion scene in 1885 when they purchased the *Lady Margaret* (1) from the ailing Bristol Channel Express Steamship Co. The suffix was not part of the name, but is necessary as three Bristol Channel ships were so named, after Lady Margaret Crichton-Stuart, the first child of the Marquis of Bute, a most prominent Cardiff citizen. This view is enhanced by the 'passengers', possibly directors and shareholders of the company, formally posed for the official photograph, who give a sense of scale to the 140ft vessel.

Ilfracombe in 1889, with the excursion trade gathering momentum. At the face of the pier are, on the left, Edwards, Robertson & Co.'s new ship *Lady Gwendoline*, delivered in July 1889, and alongside, her great rival the *Waverley*. Next to the *Waverley* is Edwards, Robertson & Co.'s *Lady Margaret* (2), formerly the Clyde steamer *Carrick Castle*, which replaced the first *Lady Margaret* in 1888. On the outside of the group is the paddle tug *Privateer*, of Swansea, and, at the Stone Bench, the Cardiff paddle tug *Earl of Dunraven*.

The *Waverley* leaving Penarth in the early 1890s. This is one of the 'On Board' series of tinted postcards of the Campbell steamers which were issued in considerable numbers in the years before the First World War.

The *Ravenswood* at Ilfracombe in 1892. P&A Campbell's new steamer was built by S. McKnight & Co. of Ayr and was launched in April 1891 by Peter and Alec's sister, Isabella. Her maiden trip, from Bristol to Chepstow, took place on 3 July 1891, after which she was mainly employed on the Bristol to Ilfracombe route.

The *Lorna Doone* leaving Ilfracombe in the 1890s. Like the Campbells, Edwards, Robertson & Co. took delivery of their new steamer in July 1891. Both the *Ravenswood* and *Lorna Doone* were fairly evenly matched and racing between destinations ensued immediately – a somewhat hazardous form of rivalry which incurred the wrath of many passengers and generated much correspondence in the local press. Both companies strenuously denied such practices!

The *Westward Ho* at Bristol, 1894. Despite the intense competition with Edwards, Robertson & Co., the White Funnel steamers were rapidly establishing themselves as the superior fleet. In 1894 and the following two years the company took delivery of three new steamers very much in advance of any other in the channel. Instead of having open foredecks, they were plated in to the bows with forward saloons, and their bridges, instead of spanning the paddle boxes aft of the funnels, were placed forward. The first of this famous trio of sister ships is seen at Hotwells Landing Stage during the first months of her service, with the *Lorna Doon* astern.

The cover of the Bristol Channel & District Guide of 1895. This publication was first issued in 1893 and appeared annually until 1939, except during the war years. It contained a considerable amount of information about the company, its ships and their ports of call, and was particularly good value for money!

The *Cambria* on trials in the Firth of Clyde, 24 May 1895. The second ship of the trio was built by H. McIntyre of Alloa. After her launch she was towed around the north of Scotland for fitting out at the yard of Guybon Hutson in Glasgow before running her maiden trip from Bristol to Ilfracombe on Saturday 1 June 1895.

The *Britannia* at Bristol, 1896. The final member of the trio was undoubtedly the best – the experience gained in the building and running of the *Westward Ho* and *Cambria* was put into practice in the *Britannia*. In speed and manoeuvrability she was unsurpassed and became the finest example of her type of steamer. Capt. Peter played a major part in her design and construction and commanded her for many years before the First World War. She was often referred to as 'Captain Peter's toy'.

The *Britannia* leaving Bristol, 1896. With an increasing number of steamers sailing from Bristol, the landing stage at Hotwells, just upstream from the Clifton Suspension Bridge, was proving inadequate and had to be extended. The work is nearing completion as a group of Victorian bystanders watch the departure of the *Britannia* for an evening cruise.

A busy day at Ilfracombe in the mid-1890s. Ilfracombe became the Mecca for Bristol Channel excursions and quickly became transformed from a quiet fishing village into a major holiday resort. The steamers berthed here at the pier are, from left to right: Edwards, Robertson & Co.'s *Bonnie Doon*, *Lorna Doone* and *Scotia*, Campbell's *Westward Ho* and *Cambria*, and Pockett's *Brighton*. The last-named vessel, built originally for the Newhaven to Dieppe service in 1878, came to the Bristol Channel in 1894 and was employed almost exclusively on the Swansea to Ilfracombe service with occasional visits to Lynmouth, Lundy Island and Clovelly.

The *Lady Margaret* (3) leaving Penarth in the 1890s. Faced with the superior Campbell competition, Edwards, Robertson & Co. went out of business at the end of 1895. Towards the end of the century the Campbells had the Bristol Channel virtually to themselves. No less than seven ships joined the fleet within eight years. The first was the *Lady Margaret*, built in 1895 originally to the order of Edwards, Robertson & Co. but transferred to the Lady Margaret Steamship Co. before her launch. After only one season she was sold to the White Funnel fleet in 1896.

The *Glen Rosa* at Barry. Built in 1877, the *Glen Rosa* was a much-travelled steamer, having sailed on the Clyde, the Thames and on the South Coast. She was purchased by Capt. Alec in 1897 on his own account and sold to the limited company in the following year. She is shown at the newly opened Barry pier in 1899.

PS. Bonnie Doon

The *Bonnie Doon* at Newport, *c.*1900. Another widely travelled steamer, the former Edwards, Robertson & Co. ship was originally from the Clyde where, owing to frequent mechanical trouble, she had earned the nickname 'Bonnie Breakdoon'. During her period in the Bristol Channel, however, she appears to have been a reliable and useful vessel. P&A Campbell Ltd purchased her in 1899.

The *Scotia* off Portishead; this former Glasgow & South Western Railway steamer had joined the Edwards, Robertson fleet in 1893. With her unusual profile and antiquated appearance, she looked somewhat out of place alongside other members of the Campbell fleet, which she joined in 1899.

The *Albion* in the River Usk. Launched in 1893 for the Belfast and County Down Railway, the *Slieve Donard* served the ports and resorts of Northern Ireland until she was purchased by Campbells in 1899, who renamed her *Albion*. She ran in the Bristol Channel during that season but was to spend the following three years assisting in the development of the company's South Coast operations.

The *Britannia* at Newport, *c.*1900. The flags flown by the 'Brit' may commemorate a special occasion or simply a charter trip, such as a factory outing. Such events were a common feature in the years long before the advent of paid annual leave. The employees would contribute a small sum each week and hoped that the sun would shine on the 'big day'.

The *Westward Ho* at Chepstow in the early 1900s. Before the First World War the Monmouthshire town of Chepstow was a frequent port of call. The original landing facilities, pictured, consisted of a moored barge, used as a landing stage, joined to the river bank by a wooden bridge. This rather primitive arrangement was replaced by a new pier in 1907.

ROYAL VICTORIA PIER, TENBY.

The *Britannia* leaving Tenby in the 1900s. The excursion steamers had called at Tenby since the early 1890s, berthing at the harbour wall until 1899, when the Royal Victoria pier was opened by the Duke and Duchess of York.

The *Westward Ho* outward bound from Bristol in the 1900s.

Horse-drawn cabs await steamer passengers at Ilfracombe pier, *c.*1903. The *Britannia* lies at the Stone Bench with the *Cambria* alongside.

Ilfracombe from Hillsborough in the early 1900s. The view from Hillsborough commands a magnificent panorama, not only of the harbour and the town but, on a clear day, as far as Lundy in the west and South Wales in the north. The *Brighton* is about to take the pier but the *Britannia* is just leaving the Stone Bench. The *Brighton* has therefore started backing out to give the *Britannia* a clear passage into the channel.

THE STEWARD'S DEPARTMENT.

The Steward's Department is a special feature in the steamers of P. and A. Campbell, Limited. "Equal to any first-class Hotel and not so dear."—"South Wales Daily News."

"Regular sea-trippers hardly need to be told that supplemented by the attention, civility, and good catering for which Messrs. P. & A. Campbell are so well known, and the presence of the superior company one usually meets on board their steamers, a trip down Channel will at all times prove a matter of pleasure and enjoyment."

("Bristol Times and Mirror.")

"The table was more than liberal, the management simply perfect, and the convenience of those on board consulted in every possible way."

PRICE LIST.

SERVED IN THE DINING SALOONS.

Breakfast, with fish, ham and eggs, etc.	2	0
Luncheons, soup, cold salmon, cold meat, etc.	2	0
Dinner, soup, fish, meat, vegetables, etc.	2	6
Tea, with fish, cold salmon, meat, toast, etc	2	0
Tea, with fish or meat	1	6
Tea, plain, with preserves, etc.	1	0

SUNDRIES.

Cup of tea, with bread or biscuits	6d.
Coffee, ditto	6d.
Sandwiches	4d.
Bovril, per cup	3d.
Biscuits and cheese	6d.
Plate of meat and potatoes	1/-

WINES, SPIRITS, and CIGARS of the FINEST QUALITY.

CHOCOLATE of the following Manufacturers may be obtained on board : FRY'S, BOVRIL CO.'s, PERCY'S, and CADBURY'S.

The dining saloon tariff in the 1900s.

26

Passengers disembarking from the *Brighton* at Clovelly. Here, as well as at Lynmouth and Lundy, landing and embarking were accomplished by way of small boats that were rowed between the steamer and the beach by the local boatmen – a relatively simple operation except in a choppy sea!

Capt. Allan Livingstone on the bridge of the *Cambria*. Allan Livingstone joined P&A Campbell as an apprentice in the 1890s and was promoted 'through the ranks'. His first command was the *Waverley* but he was later transferred to the *Cambria*, the ship with which he was most closely associated until his retirement in 1926.

The *Cambria* at the breakwater, Porthcawl, in the 1900s.

The *Ravenswood* leaving the Pier Head, Cardiff, in the 1900s.

The *Gwalia* on trials in the Firth of Clyde, March 1905. The Barry Railway had been trying to obtain parliamentary sanction to run steamers in the Bristol Channel since the late 1890s. In 1904 a bill was finally passed permitting them to do so. Two magnificent sister ships, the *Gwalia* and *Devonia*, were built by John Brown of Clydebank. They began service in the spring of 1905 and brought renewed competition to the White Funnel Fleet. The Barry Railway was allowed to run steamers provided their journeys began and ended at Barry. To increase their passenger-carrying potential (by starting trips from Bristol, Newport and Cardiff) the company evaded the restriction by registering the steamers in the names of private individuals, rather than in the name of the company, all of whom were connected with the Barry Railway as directors or shareholders. The Campbells were aware of this ploy and began litigation to ensure that the terms of the bill were adhered to. Despite much prevarication, the Barry Railway eventually admitted to the deception and, from the end of July 1907, agreed to abide by the restrictions.

The *Gwalia* leaving Barry in 1905. The funnels of the Barry Railway ships were at first buff with narrow black tops and their hulls were black. However, after only a short time in service they were repainted – the hulls became light grey and their funnels a deep red with black tops, leading inevitably to the company being known as the 'Red Funnel Line'. In 1906 yet another change was made when their hulls reverted to black.

The *Westonia* at Barry Pier, 1906. The *Westonia* was yet another steamer which had 'done the rounds' of Great Britain. She had been launched in 1899 as the *Tantallon Castle* for service on the Firth of Forth. As the *Sussex Queen*, she ran on the South Coast and then operated in North Wales as the *Rhos Colwyn* before her purchase by the Barry Railway in 1905. Barry Pier station, pictured, was built specifically for the benefit of steamer passengers brought from Cardiff and the valley towns, the line being an extension from Barry Island.

The *Gwalia* at Newport, July 1905. Occasionally the steamers were called upon to perform special duties. This view shows the *Gwalia* in the entrance lock to Newport Docks, about to leave with soldiers of a Volunteer Battalion of the South Wales Borderers for their annual camp at Minehead.

The *Westonia* leads the *Westward Ho* up the River Avon, 1906.

The *Albion* aground at Portishead. On the morning of 1 April 1907 the *Albion* set off from Newport in thick fog on a day trip to Bristol. She approached the Somerset coast at a snail's pace but, before it could be seen, she had run on to the shingle beach between two rocky outcrops at Blacknore Point.

The passengers continued their journey to Bristol by road and the *Albion* was refloated that evening with the aid of tugs, little the worse for her experience.

Haymaking at Ilfracombe, *c.*1907. The view is from Quayfields, then part of a farm and now a cliff walk with a putting green and go-kart circuit. Beyond the haystack the *Britannia* berths at the pier while the *Cambria* departs and the *Albion* waits offshore.

Passengers aboard the *Westward Ho* bound for Newquay, 1907. Occasional trips were run to the Cornish port until the early 1930s. From Bristol the trip took about nine hours each way, which, with about two hours ashore at Newquay, meant a departure time of around 5 a.m., returning home around 11 p.m. Quite a day out!

The seafront at Penarth, c.1907. The *Waverley* berths at the pier while one of the Red Funnel sisters passes on her way into Cardiff.

P.S. BRITOCH4   1907 NO.B. PHILLIPSE.PHOTO

The *Britannia* arriving at Ilfracombe, 1907. On the wing of the bridge is Capt. Daniel Taylor, a Scotsman who came to the Bristol Channel with Alec Campbell in the 1890s. He rose to the rank of captain and was commodore of the Campbell fleet from 1910 until his retirement in 1927.

Birnbeck Island, Weston Super Mare, c.1908. The mainstay of all the Bristol Channel steamer services was the Cardiff to Weston 'ferry'. At times there were as many as a dozen round trips per day. It was one of the shortest and therefore cheapest of trips. In the mid-1900s a day return fare was 1/6d., each single journey taking around an hour. Many of the passengers who landed at Weston ventured no farther than Birnbeck Island, all the facilities and amusements they required being on hand.

Birnbeck Island, Weston-Super-Mare, 1908. The *Albion* lies alongside the embarkation jetty while the *Waverley* waits offshore. On the left of the photograph is the low water jetty, nearing completion prior to its opening in 1909. It was built to enable the steamers to land at any state of the tide. However, the prevailing winds and swell from the west, together with the strong tidal flow and currents, made it a difficult and sometimes dangerous berthing place, unpopular with the ships' masters. It was demolished in the winter of 1921-1922.

The *Devonia* at Penarth Pier, *c*.1908. This postcard was entitled 'A Busy Corner'.

The *Devonia* at Ilfracombe, *c*.1908.

Passengers aboard the *Westward Ho* at Ilfracombe, *c*.1908.

The *Cambria* arriving at Ilfracombe in 1908.

The *Barry* in the River Avon. In 1907 the Red Funnel Line had taken delivery of a new steamer from the yard of John Brown of Clydebank. She was launched as the *Barry* and was a most attractive steamer. Capt. Peter Campbell is said to have commented very favourably on her appearance and stated that she was a vessel which he would be happy to own. His wish was to be granted five years later.

The *Gwalia* and the *Barry* at Barry Pier, 1908-1909. The Barry Railway found themselves in financial difficulties after agreeing to begin their journeys only from Barry. The limited number of passengers carried from that port generated insufficient revenue to maintain the running of the company's steamers and they were offered for sale. The entire fleet passed into the hands of Bristol Channel Passenger Boats Ltd from June 1910. This newly formed company was without connection with the Barry Railway and the ships were therefore free to embark passengers at any port.

The *Ravenswood* leaving Ilfracombe in 1909. In the seven years prior to the First World War P&A Campbell Ltd embarked on a programme of alterations and improvements to their existing ships, and the acquisition of a new tonnage. The *Ravenswood* was re-boilered and re-engineered, appearing with one funnel and with the bridge moved forward.

The *Terra Nova* leaving Cardiff, 15 June 1910. Capt. Robert Falcon Scott sent his ship, the *Terra Nova*, to Cardiff to take on coal before setting off on what was to become his final expedition to Antarctica. Her departure was accompanied by numerous vessels including the *Ravenswood* and the *Devonia*, both of which escorted her as far as Barry.

'We don't get summers like we used to.' The old adage is often heard but the records prove otherwise: the summer of 1910, for example, was a shocker! At the end of June severe gales swept through the Bristol Channel; nevertheless, the passengers turned up and the ships sailed. Here, on 29 June 1910, the *Cambria* passes Rillage Point, about a mile east of Ilfracombe, on her way to the pier.

The *Devonia* shipping a 'green' sea near Rillage Point, 30 June 1910.

The Pier Head, Cardiff, 1910. The *Ravenswood* awaits her passengers at the pontoon, while the *Britannia* manoeuvres into position for her departure down channel.

The *Britannia* passing Pill, in the River Avon, 1910/1911. The village of Pill, on the south bank of the river, was home to many of the Bristol pilots and its annual carnival was a great occasion. Numerous events took place on the river, one of which appears to have been interrupted by the outward bound *Britannia*.

Winter quarters in the Floating Harbour, Bristol, 1910. At the end of each season the White Funnel steamers were laid up in the Bristol City Docks. As the following spring approached, they became 'hives of activity' with shipyard workers, engineers, officers and crews preparing them for the forthcoming season. In this view the *Britannia*, *Cambria* and *Albion* lie at the Mardyke Wharf. The small boat in the foreground is the Mardyke ferry, which took passengers across the harbour, thus saving a long walk round.

The *Lady Ismay* off Penarth. In 1911 P&A Campbell Ltd took delivery of the first of the three new steamers built by the Ailsa Shipbuilding Co. of Troon. They were fitted with small engines and paddle wheels with the emphasis on economy of running. They were able to carry over 1,000 passengers, and their small paddle boxes enabled five gangways to be used for a rapid turnaround at the piers. The first of these ships, the *Lady Ismay*, is seen off Penarth in her first season.

Passengers aboard the *Albion* at Ilfracombe, 11 September 1911.

Passengers aboard the *Barry* in 1911.

The second ship of the new trio was the *Glen Avon*, launched at Troon on 30 May 1912. Her maiden trip from Newport to Bristol took place on 13 July 1912. A photograph believed to have been taken on this occasion forms the centrepiece of this composite postcard, issued by Newport photographer W. Clifton.

The *Devonia* arriving at Ilfracombe, 1911. After two years competing with the White Funnel Fleet, Bristol Channel Passenger Boats Ltd found themselves in financial difficulties. While under their ownership the standard of upkeep of the vessels had deteriorated and the company finally offered them for sale. The *Gwalia* was purchased by the Furness Railway for their service between Barrow and Fleetwood; she was renamed *Lady Moyra*, after the wife of one of that company's directors. The *Devonia*, *Barry* and *Westonia* were purchased by P&A Campbell Ltd. Once again the White Funnel Fleet reigned supreme.

The *Westonia* leaving Weston.

The *Tintern* off Penarth, 1912. When they joined the Campbell fleet, the *Devonia* and *Barry* remained unchanged apart from repainting in Campbell colours. The *Westonia*, however, was completely altered and appeared with a single funnel, forward bridge and the name of *Tintern*. Photographs of her in this condition are extremely rare as she only ran in Campbell ownership for the 1912 season. She was sold to Portugal for use as a ferry across the River Tagus, no doubt as a result of an offer which Campbells' could not refuse. Once again she was renamed – *Alentejo* – her sixth name in thirty-five years!

The *Barry* arriving at Ilfracombe in 1912.

The *Devonia* arriving at Ilfracombe in 1912.

By the Magnificent Saloon Steamers of

P. & A. CAMPBELL Ltd.

BRITANNIA, WESTWARD HO! CAMBRIA, LADY ISMAY, WAVERLEY, GLEN ROSA, BARRY, DEVONIA, and GLEN AVON.

From HOTWELLS, Bristol
(Weather and Circumstances permitting)

Embarking Stage, about 30 minutes by Electric Tram from Joint Railway Station (Temple Mead), or by Taxi about 10 minutes.

THURSDAY, July 3rd.
Afternoon Trip to CHEPSTOW. Leaving at 3.30 p.m. (allowing about 1¼ hrs. on shore). Return Chepstow 6.15 p.m.
Fare 1/6 including Pier Toll (Coupon Holders 2/-).
Circular Trip to CHEPSTOW (by Boat and back by Rail). Leaving at 3.30 p.m. Fare 2/6 (including Pier Toll).
NOTE.—Passengers can book to Chepstow from any of the G.W.R. Stations in Bristol and return by Steamer at 6.15 p.m.
to Hotwells Landing Stage. Fare 2/6 (including Pier Toll).
Evening CRUISE DOWN CHANNEL towards Clevedon. Leaving at 5.15 p.m. Back about 7.15. Fare 1/-
Evening Circular Trip to CLEVEDON (by Boat and back by Rail). Leaving at 7.30 p.m.
Single Trip to CLEVEDON, PENARTH, and CARDIFF. Leaving at 7.30 p.m.
NOTE.—A Steamer leaves Cardiff at 2.30 p.m., Penarth 2.40 p.m., Clevedon 3.35 p.m., for Bristol.

FRIDAY, July 4th.
CLEVEDON ASSOCIATION FOOTBALL CLUB CARNIVAL.
CLEVEDON, WESTON, and ILFRACOMBE (calling off LYNMOUTH to and fro).
Leaving at 8.15 a.m. Return Ilfracombe 3.30 p.m., Weston 6, Clevedon 6.30.
Morning Circular Trip to CLEVEDON or WESTON (by Boat and back by Rail). Leaving at 8.15 a.m.
CARDIFF (calling CLEVEDON return journey). Leave 8.15 a.m. Return Cardiff 3.20 & 6 p.m., Clevedon 4.15 & 6.50
Evening CRUISE DOWN CHANNEL towards Clevedon. Leaving at 5.45 p.m. Back about 7.45. Fare 1/-
Single Trip to CLEVEDON and CARDIFF. Leaving at 8.30 p.m.
NOTE.—A Steamer leaves Ilfracombe 12.15 p.m. (calling off Lynmouth), Cardiff 3.20 p.m., Clevedon 4.15 p.m., for Bristol
also a Steamer leaves Cardiff at 8.30 p.m.

SATURDAY, July 5th.
Morning Cruise to CHEPSTOW. Leaving at 6.10 a.m. Back about 8.40.
Day Trip to CHEPSTOW. Leaving at 6.10 a.m. Return Chepstow 7.45 p.m. sharp. Fare 2/6
Morning Circular Trip to CHEPSTOW (by Boat & back by Rail). Leave 6.10 a.m. Fare 2/6
CLEVEDON ASSOCIATION FOOTBALL CLUB CARNIVAL.
CLEVEDON, WESTON, and ILFRACOMBE (calling off LYNMOUTH to and fro).
Leaving at 8.30 a.m. Return Ilfracombe 4 p.m., Weston 6.30, Clevedon 7.
Morning Circular Trip to CLEVEDON or WESTON (by Boat and back by Rail). Leaving at 8.30 a.m.
CARDIFF (calling at PENARTH and CLEVEDON on return journey). Leave 8.30 a.m. Return Cardiff 4.10 p.m., Penarth 4.20, Clevedon 5.15.
Evening Trip to CHEPSTOW. Leave 5.30 p.m. Allowing some time on shore. Return Chepstow 7.45 p.m. sharp.
Fare 1/6 including Pier Toll (Coupon Holders 2/-).
Evening Circular Trip to CHEPSTOW (by Boat & back by Rail). Leave 5.30 p.m. Fare 2/6 (including Pier Toll)
NOTE.—Passengers can book to Chepstow from any of the G.W.R. Stations in Bristol and return by Steamer at 7.45 p.m. sharp
to Hotwells Landing Stage. Fare 2/6 (including Pier Toll).
Evening CRUISE DOWN CHANNEL towards Clevedon. Leaving at 6.30 p.m. Back about 8.30. Fare 1/-
Single Trip to NEWPORT. Leaving at 8.15 p.m. Fare 2/-
Single Trip to CLEVEDON, PENARTH, and CARDIFF. Leaving at 9 p.m.
NOTE.—A Steamer leaves Cardiff 6.20 a.m., Penarth 6.30 a.m., Clevedon 7.30 a.m.; also a Steamer leaves Newport 6.30 a.m. & 5.15 p.m. for Bristol.

MONDAY, July 7th.
CLEVEDON, WESTON, and ILFRACOMBE (calling off LYNMOUTH to and fro).
Leaving at 9.30 a.m. Return Ilfracombe 4.15 p.m., Weston 6.45, Clevedon 7.15.
Circular Trip to CLEVEDON or WESTON (by Boat and back by Rail). Leaving at 9.30 a.m.
Evening CRUISE DOWN CHANNEL towards Clevedon. Leaving at 7.30 p.m. Back about 9.30. Fare 1/-
Single Trip to CARDIFF, PENARTH, and BARRY. Leaving at 8.30 p.m.
NOTE.—A Steamer leaves Barry at 6.45 a.m., Penarth 7.10 a.m., Cardiff 7.30 a.m., for Bristol.

TUESDAY, July 8th.
CLEVEDON, WESTON, MINEHEAD, and ILFRACOMBE (calling off LYNMOUTH to and fro).
Leaving at 8.45 a.m. Return Ilfracombe 5 p.m., Minehead 6.30, Weston 7.45, Clevedon 8.15.
Circular Trip to CLEVEDON, WESTON, or MINEHEAD (by Boat and back by Rail). Leaving at 8.45 a.m.
Evening CRUISE DOWN CHANNEL towards Clevedon. Leaving at 8 p.m. Back about 10. Fare 1/-

WEDNESDAY, July 9th.
CLEVEDON, WESTON, MUMBLES, and TENBY.)
Leaving at 8.30 a.m. Return Tenby 5 p.m., Mumbles 6.30, Weston 9.10, Clevedon 9.45.
CLEVEDON, WESTON, MINEHEAD, and ILFRACOMBE (calling off LYNMOUTH to and fro).
Leaving at 9 a.m. Return Ilfracombe 5 p.m., Minehead 6.35, Weston 7.50, Clevedon 8.25.
Circular Trips to CLEVEDON, WESTON, or MINEHEAD (by Boat and back by Rail).
Leaving at 8.30, 9 a.m., and 12.30 p.m. for Clevedon or Weston, and 9 a.m. for Minehead.
Afternoon Trip to CLEVEDON and WESTON.
Leaving at 12.30 p.m. Return Weston 6, 7.50 and 9.10 p.m., Clevedon 6.40, 8.25, and 9.45.
Evening CRUISE DOWN CHANNEL towards Clevedon. Leaving at 8 p.m. Back about 10. Fare 1/-

THURSDAY, July 10th.
CLEVEDON, WESTON, MINEHEAD, and ILFRACOMBE (calling off LYNMOUTH to and fro).
Leaving at 9.15 a.m. Return Ilfracombe 5.15 p.m., Minehead 7, Weston 8.15, Clevedon 8.50.
Circular Trip to CLEVEDON, WESTON, or MINEHEAD (by Boat and back by Rail). Leaving at 9.15 a.m.

FRIDAY, July 11th.
CLEVEDON, WESTON, MINEHEAD, and ILFRACOMBE (calling off LYNMOUTH to and fro).
Leaving at 10 a.m. Return Ilfracombe 5.45 p.m., Minehead 7.30, Weston 8.45, Clevedon 9.20.
Circular Trips to CLEVEDON, WESTON, or MINEHEAD (by Boat and back by Rail).
Leaving at 10 a.m. and 1 p.m. for Clevedon or Weston, and 10 a.m. for Minehead.
Morning CRUISE DOWN CHANNEL towards Clevedon. Leaving at 11 a.m. Back about 12.50. Fare 1/-
Afternoon Trip to CLEVEDON and WESTON. Leaving at 1 p.m. Return Weston 8.45 p.m., Clevedon 9.20.
Single Trip to PENARTH and CARDIFF (via CLEVEDON and WESTON). Leaving at 1 p.m.
NOTE.—A Steamer leaves Cardiff at 8.45 a.m., Penarth 8.55 a.m., Clevedon 9.45 a.m., for Bristol.

SATURDAY, July 12th.
CLEVEDON, WESTON, MINEHEAD, and ILFRACOMBE (calling off LYNMOUTH to and fro).
Leaving at 11 a.m. Return Ilfracombe 6.30 p.m., Minehead 8.10, Weston 9.30, Clevedon 10.10.
Circular Trips to CLEVEDON, WESTON, or MINEHEAD (by Boat and back by Rail).
Leaving at 11 a.m. and 2 p.m. for Clevedon or Weston, and 11 a.m. for Minehead.
Special Cheap Trip to MUMBLES. Leave 12.15 p.m. Return Mumbles 6.40 p.m. Return Fare—Mumbles 3/6.
Afternoon Trip to CARDIFF, PENARTH, and BARRY (for Barry Island, Whitmore Bay, &c).
Leaving at 12.15 p.m. Return Barry 8.30 p.m., Penarth 15, Cardiff 9.30.
Cheap Afternoon Trip to ILFRACOMBE (calling at CLEVEDON, WESTON, and off LYNMOUTH down trip only). Leave 2.30 p.m. Return Ilfracombe 8.30 p.m. direct to Bristol. Return Fare, this trip, to Ilfracombe 3/6
Afternoon Trip to CLEVEDON, PENARTH, and CARDIFF.
Leaving at 2.30 p.m. Return Penarth 9.5 p.m., Cardiff 9.30, Clevedon 10.10.
Afternoon Trip to CLEVEDON & WESTON. Leave 2.30 p.m. Return Weston 9.30 p.m., Clevedon 10.10.
NOTE.—A Steamer leaves Cardiff at 9.45 a.m., Penarth 9.55 a.m., Clevedon 10.50 a.m., for Bristol.

(left margin, vertical): CIRCULAR BOOKINGS to CLEVEDON and WESTON. Return Train Times up to and including Friday, July 11th (day of issue only)—from Clevedon by any Train having a through connection (except 7 p.m.); and from Weston-super-Mare (General Station) to Clifton Bridge, 3.30, 5.20, 7.45, & 8.40 p.m.: Lawrence Hill, 6 and 8.5 p.m.: St. Anne's Park, 6, 8.5, & 8.40 p.m.; Brislington, 5.20 & 8.5 p.m.; Ashley Hill, 6 & 7.10 p.m.: Clifton Bridge, 3.30, 5.20, 7.45, & 8.40 p.m.: Lawrence Hill, St. Anne's Park, and Temple Mead 7.45 and 8.40 p.m. NOTE—On and after July 12th the Return Train Times to Lawrence Hill, St. Anne's Park, and Temple Mead will be 6, 7.45, and 8.40 p.m.: Bedminster 7.45 and 8.40 p.m. Passengers desiring to return by Rail must state so when purchasing Tickets on board Steamer, and mention to which Station they wish to return.

(right margin, vertical): Average Passage from Bristol to (Clevedon :: Weston :: 1 hour :: Cardiff or Newport 2 hours :: Lynmouth Ilfracombe :: 4 hours :: 1¼ :: 2 :: 4½)

FARES FROM BRISTOL TO

	Single.	Day Return.	Tourist.
Clevedon or Weston ...	1/6	2/-	3/-
Cardiff or Penarth ...	2/-	2/6	3/6
Barry (Including Pier Toll at Barry) ...	2/-	2/6 (COUPON HOLDERS 3/-)	
Minehead ...	3/6	4/-	
Lynmouth or Ilfracombe ...	4/-	5/-	Week-end (Fri. or Sat. to Mon. or Tues.) 6/-
(Lynmouth Fares do not include landing or embarking)			
Mumbles ...	4/-	5/-	
Tenby ...		6/6	
Clovelly (Including landing and embarking)		6/6	

Clevedon or Weston (Down by Boat and back by Rail) 2/- Minehead (Down by Boat and back by Rail) 5/3
Children under 12 years, half price. Dogs, Bicycle, Prams, or Mail Carts (at Owner's risk), 1/- each way. Motor Bicycles (at Owner's risk), 2/- each way. The Company reserve the right to alter the advertised times or withdraw any of the above sailings, as Weather and other circumstances may require. A reasonable quantity of passenger's Luggage carried free of charge (at Owner's risk). Passengers are requested to label same. Special Terms made with Picnic Parties, Clubs, &c. Breakfasts, Dinners, and Teas can be had on Board at Moderate Terms. "Bristol Channel District Guide," Official Handbook of P. & A. CAMPBELL Ltd., 300 Illustrations, a mass of interesting matter—Price 4d., per Post 7d. A limited number of Half-Fare Coupon Books, 10/- (not transferable), will be issued, for NEW CONDITIONS and further particulars apply to T. COOK & SON, 49 Corn Street; on board the Steamers, or at the Company's Office, 1 Britannia Buildings, Cumberland Basin.
Telegraphic Addresses :—"Ravenswood, Bristol." "Ravenswood, Cardiff."
Telephone Nos.—3112 Bristol. 789 Cardiff. 44 Weston. 37 Ilfracombe. 46 Lynmouth. 560 Newport. 17 Clevedon.

A Bristol Channel timetable for 1913.

The *Britannia* in the Floating Harbour, Bristol, 1913. Following the *Titanic* disaster in April 1912, the Board of Trade issued regulations for radical changes with regard to increases in life-saving apparatus carried by all passenger ships. As part of those measures all, of the Campbell steamers were fitted with either one or two extra lifeboats, depending on the size of the vessel. In this view the *Britannia* has received her additional lifeboats, forward of the paddle boxes.

The *Glen Usk* on trials on the measured mile, off Skelmorlie, in the Firth of Clyde, 27 May 1914. The third of the Ailsa-built ships was launched in 1914 as the *Glen Usk*. As with the *Westward Ho/Cambria/Britannia* trio, each vessel was an improvement on her predecessor. The design and building of the *Glen Usk* was supervised by Capt. Dan Taylor and the shipbuilders produced an undoubted 'masterpiece'.

The *Glen Usk* at Newport during her first season.

Two

The South Coast before the First World War

The *Cambria* at Ryde Pier at the turn of the century. The Campbells expanded their services in 1897 with excursions from the Hampshire coast. The *Cambria* was the principal steamer, supported by either the *Glen Rosa* or *Albion*. Running mainly from Southampton, the sailings extended from Swanage to Brighton, including the Isle of Wight, with regulars trips to Cherbourg and occasional visits to Boulogne.

The venture was reasonably successful but towards the end of 1901 an even more attractive proposition presented itself. The Brighton, Worthing & South Coast Steamboat Co. placed their two widely contrasting steamers on the market. The Sussex coast, like the Bristol Channel, was an area ripe for development and the Campbells were just the people to do it! The *Brighton Queen*, seen here on trials in the Clyde in 1897, was purchased by Peter and Alec on their own account. She was altered 'Campbell fashion' at considerable expense and began running from Brighton in 1902.

The *Princess May* at Bristol, 1902. The brothers did not want the Brighton Co.'s second steamer, but the deal was for 'both or neither'. The *Princess May* was similarly bought privately and brought up to Campbell standard. After a short spell in the Bristol Channel, she went to the South Coast. Here she attracted the attention of an Italian shipowner who considered her ideal for his company's services in the Bay of Naples. Accordingly, without having joined the limited company, she was sold later that season.

The *Brighton Queen* arriving at the West Pier, Brighton, in the 1900s. The company abandoned the Southampton base from 1903 and transferred its South Coast headquarters to Brighton. The *Brighton Queen* was purchased by the limited company that year and became a great favourite of Sussex residents and holidaymakers. She sailed to France regularly and there were few accessible places between Swanage and Ramsgate at which she did not call.

The *Brighton Queen* at Boulogne in the early 1900s.

The *Brighton Queen* was the principal Sussex steamer until the First World War and took most of the longer sailings. She was, however, supported by various smaller vessels which ran the shorter, coastal cruises. One of the small vessels, the *Glen Rosa*, is seen here leaving Eastbourne in 1904.

The *Brighton Queen* at Cowes, Isle of Wight, in the early 1900s. Alongside her is the *Brodick Castle*, owned by Cosens of Weymouth.

A view of the Quay Gambetta at Boulogne, with the *Brighton Queen* tucked into her berth.

The *Brighton Queen* leaving Boulogne in the 1900s.

One of the most appealing features of the paddle steamers was the white wake which trailed behind them. The *Brighton Queen* shows this off to great advantage as she leaves Brighton in the 1900s.

SPECIAL NOTICE!

MONDAY, AUGUST 20th.

The Magnificent Express Steamers

Brighton Queen
and Bonnie Doon

Will leave Eastbourne Pier (weather and circumstances permitting) as under :—

P.S. BRIGHTON QUEEN

9.0 a.m. To BRIGHTON and

BOURNEMOUTH

Allowing 2 hours at Bournemouth or 9½ hours at Brighton.

NOTE ! The Trip to Bournemouth is especially attractive, passing *en route* Brighton, Worthing, Littlehampton, Bognor, Selsea, Bembridge, Ryde, Portsmouth, Southsea, The Spithead Forts, Southampton Water, Cowes, Hurst Castle, The Needles, &c.

Returning from Bournemouth 4.15 p.m. ; Brighton West Pier 8.0 p.m. ; Brighton Palace Pier 8.15 p.m. ; Back 9.30 p.m.

Return Fares : BOURNEMOUTH 7/6 ; BRIGHTON 2/6*

P.S. BONNIE DOON

9.30 a.m. To HASTINGS,
Morning Return 1/6 ; Day Return 2/-*
Returning from Hastings at 11.0 or 3.0

12.15 p.m. To HASTINGS, Return 2/-*
Returning from Hastings at 3.0.

4.15 p.m. To BRIGHTON, Return 2/-*
Allowing 2.0 hours ashore, returning by " Brighton Queen " from Brighton West Pier, 8.0 p.m., Palace Pier, 8.15 p.m.

*With Railway Facilities.
Children under 12 years of age, half-price.

CATERING IN CAMPBELL'S WELL KNOWN STYLE

For further particulars apply—P. & A. CAMPBELL, Ltd.
Telephone 117y.   PIER, EASTBOURNE

CHRISTIAN, PRINTER, EASTBOURNE.

An Eastbourne timetable from 1906.

All went well with the South Coast services until 1908, when a rival steamer, the *Lady Rowena*, was chartered to run on Campbell territory between Brighton, Eastbourne and Hastings. The brothers dealt with the 'intruder' by sending one of their superior vessels to sail in competition with her and letting the public decide which they preferred. Accordingly, the *Cambria* left the Bristol Channel for the South Coast on 31 August 1908. Her trip 'around the land' coincided with a severe gale and mountainous seas.

Fortunately, one of the few passengers aboard had taken his camera and, despite the difficult conditions, has left to posterity a record of that terrifying journey. The photographs shown here were taken off Start Point, South Devon, while the ship had stopped in order for the engineers to clear the paddles of pit props, washed off the deck of a ship which had passed earlier. The *Cambria* arrived at Southampton on the following day with much superficial damage, but was soon at work from Brighton. The Campbells' ploy was a success; passengers flocked to the *Cambria* and the defeated *Lady Rowena* left the South Coast at the end of the season.

An Eastbourne timetable from 1908.

1908

Friday, September 4th.

PLEASURE SAILINGS
From EASTBOURNE PIER
(Weather and Circumstances permitting).

P.S. 'Bonnie Doon'

11.40 a.m. Round the Royal Sovereign Lightship

Back 1 p.m. sharp **Fare 1/- Children, 6d.**

2.45 to **Hastings** Single 1/- Return 1/6

Returning at once, back 5 p.m., or allowing 2¾ hours ashore, returning by "Brighton Queen," 6.30 p.m.

P.S. 'Cambria'

10.30 a.m. To **Hastings** - 1/6 Return

Leave Hastings 11.30, 2.50, 3.50 or 6.30

12.30 p.m. To **Hastings** - 1/6 Return

Leave Hastings at 2.50, 3.50 or 6.30

3.50 p.m. Grand Channel Cruise towards Newhaven Breakwater

Back 5.15 p.m. **Fare 1/-; Children 6d.**

5.15 p.m. To **Hastings** Cheap Return 1/-

Allowing short time ashore, returning by "Brighton Queen" at 6.30

P.S. 'Brighton Queen'

11.20 a.m. To **Hastings and DOVER** 2 Hours Ashore

Returning from Dover at 4.10, and from Hastings at 2.50, 3.50 or 6.30

Return Fares—**Dover 4/-, Hastings 1/6**

P. & A. CAMPBELL, Ltd., Pier, Eastbourne. Tele. 117y

CHRISTIAN, PRINTER, EASTBOURNE.

The *Cambria* returned to the Bristol Channel at the end of September. On one of her last trips to Ilfracombe, a presentation was made to Capt. Livingstone by several passengers who had been aboard on the rough trip, as a token of their appreciation of the way in which he had handled his ship. This photograph was taken on that occasion – Capt. Livingstone is seated in the centre of the second row from the front.

The *Brighton Queen* at the Palace Pier, Brighton, in the 1900s.

Fishermen on the Palace Pier, Brighton, watch the departure of the *Glen Rosa* for Newhaven at the end of her day's sailings, complete with canvas awning over her after deck.

South Parade Pier, Southsea, with the *Brighton Queen* at the jetty.

The *Bonnie Doon* leaving Eastbourne in the late 1900s.

The officers and crew of the *Bonnie Doon*. Capt. Hector McFadyen is seated in the centre of the middle row.

Hastings Pier in the 1900s. The *Glen Rosa* is at the jetty while the Hastings, St Leonards & Eastbourne Steamboat Co.'s *Cynthia* departs.

The *Brighton Queen* at Eastbourne, 1911.

The *Waverley* at Eastbourne, 1911.

The *Ravenswood* leaving Eastbourne in 1912.

Capt. David James on the bridge of the *Albion*, at Eastbourne, about to depart on the 5 p.m. sailing to Brighton.

The *Brighton Queen*, with her newly fitted forward lifeboats, arriving at Eastbourne in 1913.

The *Ravenswood* leaving Brighton, 1914. In July of 1914 the British Grand Fleet assembled in Spithead for the Royal Naval Review. Prior to assembly, various squadrons visited a variety of resorts for inspection by the public. The First Battle Squadron anchored off Brighton and the steamers were kept very busy ferrying passengers out to board the ships. The *Ravenswood* is seen here on such a duty. After the review the Fleet was instructed not to disperse. Within two weeks it was at war.

The *Brighton Queen* leaving Brighton for war service, 30 September 1914. For many of the steamers of the White Funnel Fleet, the 1914 season ended early following the outbreak of war on 4 August. A major problem facing the Royal Navy was the extent of German minelaying around the coast. Although trawlers were quickly pressed into service as minesweepers, their numbers were inadequate. Consideration was given to the possibility of using paddle steamers and, to this end, the Admiralty requisitioned the *Devonia* and *Brighton Queen* and sent them on trials. They proved more than adequate for the task and became the first of many excursion vessels to fly the White Ensign.

The *Duchess of Devonshire* arriving at Weston. In 1917 the *Glen Rosa* and *Waverley*, which had maintained the Cardiff to Weston service during the previous two seasons, were requisitioned by the Admiralty. In order to continue the ferry, the company used the *Duchess of Devonshire* for the summers of 1917, 1918 and part of 1919. Chartered from the Devon Dock, Pier & Steamship Co. of Exmouth, she was commanded by Capt. Dan Taylor and manned by other P&A Campbell personnel who had been found unsuitable for naval service.

The *Albion* at Bristol on her return from war service, February 1919. During the course of the war both the *Brighton Queen* and *Lady Ismay* had been sunk by enemy mines. The surviving steamers returned to civilian service in 1919 and 1920, apart from the *Glen Rosa*, *Waverley* and *Albion*, which were beyond economical repair and broken up. However, the *Albion*'s engines were still in near perfect condition; they were removed in Troon and held in store for installation in the company's new vessel, ordered from the Ailsa Shipbuilding Co. in October 1919.

Three

The Bristol Channel between the Wars

The *Lady Moyra* and *Devonia* off Clovelly. With the resumption of their post-war sailings, Campbells were immediately faced with competition from the Yellow Funnel Fleet – the Cardiff company of W.H. Tucker & Sons. Their two paddle steamers were purchased from the Furness Railway. One of them, the *Lady Moyra*, was an old adversary of the White Funnel Fleet – the former Barry Railway steamer, *Gwalia*. Once again racing ensued, particularly between the *Lady Moyra* and her sister ship, *Devonia*, although it appears that the honours were fairly equally divided.

The first White Funnel sailing from Swansea. Prior to the war, Swansea had been the domain of Pockett's *Brighton*. She had been sold to Turkish owners after naval service in the Dardanelles and the city was now without a steamer service. Capt. Alec, however, stepped smartly in, and the *Barry* began the company's long standing association with the Welsh port on Saturday 22 May 1920.

W. H. TUCKER & Co., Ltd.
YELLOW FUNNEL FLEET

1919   PLEASURE SAILINGS   1919

(Weather and other circumstances permitting)

From ILFRACOMBE AND LYNMOUTH by the Magnificent Saloon Steamers

'LADY MOYRA' & 'LADY EVELYN.'

Tuesday, Aug. 12th	### Trip to CLOVELLY Leaving Lynmouth 11-50 a.m. ILFRACOMBE 12-30 p.m. Returning from Clovelly 4-15 p.m. RETURN FARES from ILFRACOMBE **5/6**. Lynmouth **7/—** Including Landing and Embarking at Clovelly. Children under 12 at Half Fare. **Single Trip to Lynmouth, Minehead & Cardiff** Leaving Ilfracombe at 5-30 p.m., off Lynmouth 6-5, Minehead 7-15 p.m. for Cardiff Direct. Steamer Leaves Cardiff 9-20 a.m., Minehead 10-45, off Lynmouth 11-50 for Ilfracombe and Clovelly.
Wednesday Aug. 13th	### Trip to CLOVELLY Leaving Lynmouth 11-50 a.m., ILFRACOMBE 12-30. Returning from Clovelly at 4-15 p.m. RETURN FARES from ILFRACOMBE **5/6**. LYNMOUTH **7/—** Including Landing and Embarking at Clovelly. Children Under 12 Years of Age at Half Fare. NOTE.—Passengers by the Yellow Funnel Steamer have the Longest Time at Clovelly. **Single Trip to Lynmouth, Minehead & Cardiff** Leaving Ilfracombe 5-30 p.m. off Lynmouth 6-5 p.m., Minehead 7-15. for Cardiff. Steamer leaves Cardiff 9-20 a.m., Minehead 10-45, off Lynmouth 11-50 for Ilfracombe and Clovelly.
Thursday, Aug. 14th	### Trip to CLOVELLY Leaving Lynmouth 11-50, ILFRACOMBE PIER 12-30. Returning from Clovelly 4-15 p.m. RETURN FARES from ILFRACOMBE **5/6**. Lynmouth **7/-** including Landing and Embarking at Clovelly. Children under 12 Half Fare. **Single Trip to Lynmouth, Minehead and Cardiff** Leaving Ilfracombe 5-30 p.m., off Lynmouth 6-5, Minehead 7-15 for Cardiff. Steamer leaves Cardiff 9-20 a.m., Minehead 10-45, off Lynmouth 11-50 for Ilfracombe.
Friday, Aug. 15th	### Trip to CLOVELLY Leaving Lynmouth 11-50 a.m., ILFRACOMBE 12-30. Returning from Clovelly 4-15 p.m. RETURN FARES from ILFRACOMBE **5/6**. Lynmouth **7/—** Including Landing and Embarking at Clovelly. Children under 12 years at Half Fare. **Single Trip to Lynmouth, Minehead, & Cardiff** Leaving Ilfracombe 5-30 p.m. off Lynmouth 6-5 Minehead 7-15, for Cardiff. Steamer leaves Cardiff 9-20 a.m., Minehead 10-45, off Lynmouth 11-50, for Ilfracombe.
Saturday, Aug. 16th	### Trip to CLOVELLY Leaving Lynmouth 11-50 a.m., ILFRACOMBE PIER 12-30 p.m. Returning from Clovelly 4-15 p.m. RETURN FARES from ILFRACOMBE **5/6**. Lynmouth **7/-** including Landing and Embarking at Clovelly. Children under 12 Half Fare. ☞ (Special Rates for Parties). **Single Trip to Lynmouth, Minehead & Cardiff** Leaving Ilfracombe 5-30 p.m., off Lynmouth 6-5, Minehead 7-15, for Cardiff Steamer leaves Cardiff 9-20 a.m. Minehead 10-45, off Lynmouth 11-50 for Ilfracombe and Clovelly.

VISITORS PLEASE NOTE. Tickets for Excursions by the Yellow Funnel Steamers are not obtainable from the man in the street, or any tout

Book your Tickets at the Office, Pierville, Broad Street, or at
☞ MEREDITH'S MUSIC SALOONS, THE ARCADE. ☜

FARES :
From ILFRACOMBE to CLOVELLY, **5/6** Single or Return (including landing and embarking at Clovelly).
" ILFRACOMBE to LYNMOUTH, **5/-** Single or Return (including landing and embarking at Lynmouth).
" ILFRACOMBE or LYNMOUTH—To MINEHEAD, **5/6** Single, CARDIFF **6/-** Single, **10/-** Tourist.
" LYNMOUTH to CLOVELLY, **7/-** Single or Return (including landing and embarking at Clovelly).
Bicycles, Prams, Mail Carts (at owner's risk) **1/6** each single journey.
" LYNMOUTH TO ILFRACOMBE, **5/-** Single or Return (including landing and embarking at Lynmouth).

IMPORTANT NOTICES. The Company cannot convey Motor Cycles or Dogs under any circumstances. Passengers must strictly limit luggage. The Company do not hold themselves responsible to sail at the advertised times, but will use every endeavour to carry out the sailings. A reasonable quantity of luggage carried free at Owner's risk: passengers are requested to label same. For further particulars apply to

W. H. TUCKER & Co., Ltd., 1 Stuart Street, Cardiff, or
W. JONES, Agent, Carlton Cafe, High Street, Ilfracombe,
or at the Office (Pierville), Broad Street.

Telegrams: "Link," Cardiff.

J. H. A. ... Northfield Rd., Ilfracombe.

A Yellow Funnel Fleet timetable from 1919.

H.M. The King at Swansea.

1920

P. & A. CAMPBELL Ltd.

White Funnel Fleet

SPECIAL SAILINGS From Minehead

(Weather and other circumstances permitting)

Saturday,

July 17

ILFRACOMBE

(Calling off LYNMOUTH)

Grand Cruise to Warships in Swansea Bay

Leave Minehead **10.40** a.m.

Return Ilfracombe **7** p.m.

Weather permitting, Passengers will be allowed to go on Board one of H.M. Warships, for which Special Permission has been given.

Single Trip to Cardiff.

Leave Minehead 8.15 p.m.

NOTE—Steamer leaves Cardiff 9.30 a.m. this day for Minehead

FARES—Cruise 8s.; Ilfracombe or Lynmouth (not including Landing or Embarking) Return 5s. 6d., Single 4s. 6d.; Cardiff, Single 4s. 6d.

Further Particulars of H. KINGSBURY, Agent, Minehead and Watchet.

Cox, Printers, Minehead.

A Minehead timetable from 1920. In mid-July King George V and Queen Mary visited Swansea. Their arrival in the Royal Yacht, *Victoria and Albert*, was accompanied by the battleships *Queen Elizabeth*, *Barham*, *Malaya*, *Valiant* and *Warspite*. The Campbells made full use of the occasion and ran many special sailings to enable passengers to view and board the warships.

The *Barry* at the low-water pier, Weston, 1920.

The *Devonia* off Lundy in wet and windy weather. The disembarking of passengers in boats was normally accomplished without difficulty. However, in fresh weather, as on this occasion, extra muscle-power was needed to manoeuvre the boats safely to the beach. The vessel anchored near the *Devonia* is the MV *Lerina*, the regular Lundy packet which sailed between the island and Bideford from 1919 to 1950.

The *Westward Ho*, with her funnel removed, being re-boilered at the yard of A&J Inglis, Pointhouse, Glasgow in June-July 1920.

The *Westward Ho* at Princes Pier, Greenock, 9 July 1921, leaving for trials after re-boilering.

The launch of the *Glen Gower* at Troon, 14 February 1922. The building of Campbell's new steamer, ordered in October 1919, was seriously delayed owing to shortages of materials and a series of shipyard strikes. The Ailsa Shipbuilding Co., nevertheless, produced another fine ship – an enlarged and improved *Glen Usk*.

The *Glen Gower* being towed to the fitting-out berth.

The *Glen Gower* being fitted out.

The *Glen Gower* on trials in the Firth of Clyde, 24 May 1922. After her launch by Mrs Ethel Campbell, Alec's wife, the ship was quickly fitted out. On her trials she reached a mean speed of 17½ knots, half a knot faster than the guaranteed speed. Her Master, Capt. Duncan Smith, described her as 'a very comfortable ship.'

The *Glen Gower* arriving at Ilfracombe, 1922. The new steamer began service on the Swansea to Ilfracombe route on 3 June 1922. The summer, from mid-June, was one of continual gales, but the new ship proved herself well able to withstand the heavy seas often encountered on that exposed crossing. She experienced her first gale on 8 July; the above photograph is believed to have been taken on that occasion. Capt. Smith recorded: 'Glen Gower – very good sea-boat. Behaved splendidly and shipped no water.'

The engine room of the *Lady Moyra*. At the end of 1922, W.H. Tucker & Sons went out of business. Once again the Campbell supremacy could not be broken. Tuckers' two paddle steamers joined the White Funnel Fleet, the *Lady Evelyn* destined for the South Coast and the *Lady Moyra* remaining in the Bristol Channel.

The *Lady Moyra* arriving at Barry in tow, Thursday 23 August 1923. Her first season with Campbell was reasonably successful despite the atrocious weather, but came to an abrupt end on the night of Wednesday 22 August, when she was backing out of Ilfracombe in yet another gale. Her stern fell into a deep trough and the huge sea which followed washed over her, causing extensive damage to her rudder and steering gear. She drifted up-channel and anchored in sheltered water off Combe Martin overnight. By the early hours of the following morning, two Cardiff tugs had reached her and they began the long tow to Barry. Repairs were carried out during the course of the following winter.

Capt. Duncan Smith with the officers and crew of the *Glen Usk*. Capt. Smith is third from right in the front row. On his left is Chief Officer (later Captain) Frederick Nunn and on his right, Chief Engineer Robert Wilson.

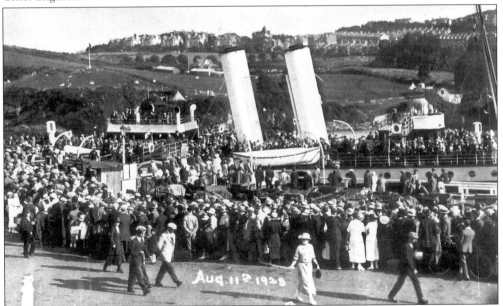

The *Glen Gower* at Ilfracombe, Saturday 11 August 1923, one of the rare fine days of that summer! Saturdays were busy days for the Swansea steamer: there were often three or four crossings to Ilfracombe, with the ship completing her sailings in the early hours of Sunday morning. The trips were combined with rail connections from the towns of South and Mid-Wales, as well as Devon and Cornwall, and catered specifically for those journeying to and from their holiday destinations. The queue of waiting travellers indicates the volume of passengers carried.

Passengers aboard the *Glen Usk* at Ilfracombe in the 1920s.

MONDAY 27 (208-157) Gale of Wly wind, plenty of Sea. Heavy rain till late afternoon.

Britannia — Locked out. Bristol to Clevedon, Cardiff, Penarhead, & Lynmouth & Ilfracombe at 10.0 am = 194 =
D. Taylor   didn't call.   didn't go beyond Cardiff.
✓ Return Cardiff 9.0 pm Clevedon 9.50 and Bristol 10.33 p.m. & into Basin.
didn't call.

Westward Ho Lying in Cumberland Basin 9.30 am Trip to Clevedon, Weston Ilfracombe & Lundy : Cancelled.
J. Ashford

Cambria Left Cardiff 9.35 am but didn't proceed any further than Barry.
Lingstone

Lady Moyra Left Cardiff 7.45 am for Ilfracombe & Newquay but returned
G. Riddell

Beverley Left Cardiff 8.0 am for Weston but had to return, remaining Trips Cancelled.
H. McFadgen

Glen Avon All Ferry Trips Cancelled.
H. Chidgey

Glen Usk Left Newport for Weston at 9.30 am but had to return.
W. Morris

Glen Gower Lying at Swansea Trip cancelled.
D. Smith

Devonia, Brighton Belle & Ravenswood. Trips cancelled. SWly Gale & Rain.
W. A. Cross,   B. A. Hawken.   F. C. Deeks.

A page from the company's memorandum book for 1925. All sailings, both in the Bristol Channel and to the South Coast, were either cancelled or curtailed.

The *Cambria* aground, 12 July 1926. Despite the treacherous nature of the Bristol Channel, the excursion steamers hold a remarkably accident-free record. Those mishaps which did occur were usually the consequence of fog. One such accident involved the *Cambria* when she slid on to the rocks at Rillage Point in 1926. Of her 146 passengers, some climbed on to the rocks and walked a mile or so to Ilfracombe while others were taken into the harbour by the ship's lifeboats or by the Ilfracombe boatmen. The *Cambria* floated off the rocks on the next high tide with little more damage than paint scraped off her hull.

The *Lady Moyra* leaving Swansea, c.1927.

A quiet day on the River Usk as the *Glen Usk* approaches the Newport Transporter Bridge. Opened in 1906, the bridge has been renovated in recent years and once more carries passengers and vehicles across the river.

Capt. Dan Taylor on the bridge of the *Britannia* at Ilfracombe in the 1920s.

A day of torrential rain at Swansea. Her trips cancelled, the *Ravenswood* heads down the River Tawe to return to Cardiff.

Another wet day at Ilfracombe. The *Glen Usk* lies at the Stone Bench and is seen from the *Glen Gower*, which, having lain alongside her, manoeuvres stern first around the face of the pier and into the channel.

Sunshine at last! The *Glen Gower* arrives at Ilfracombe during Regatta week in 1928.

The *Cambria* has her funnel painted while off service at Barry, 1932.

P. & A. CAMPBELL LTD.

SAILINGS FROM **PORTHCAWL**
By the Magnificent Saloon Steamers,

"LADY MOYRA," &c.

(Weather and Circumstances Permitting)

JULY, 1929.

THURSDAY, **JULY 18th**	**LONG AFTERNOON CHANNEL CRUISE AROUND** ## THE SCARWEATHER LIGHTSHIP LEAVING PORTHCAWL 3.35 p.m. Arriving back about 5.10 p.m. Special Fare 1s. 6d. (Children under 14 Half-price). NOTE.—Passengers having **small parcels of books or newspapers for the Crew of the Lightship** will see them put on board (weather permitting). **SINGLE TRIP TO SWANSEA, MUMBLES and ILFRACOMBE** Leaving Porthcawl 5.20 p.m. Fares.—Swansea or Mumbles 2s.6d. Ilfracombe 5s. NOTE.—Steamer leaves Swansea 2.35 p.m. for Porthcawl.
TUESDAY, **JULY 23rd**	**SPECIAL CHEAP** ## CHANNEL CRUISE AROUND THE BAYS LEAVING PORTHCAWL 8.15 p.m. Arriving back about 9.40 p.m. **Note: Special Fare 1s.** Children under 14 half-price. **SINGLE TRIP TO SWANSEA** Leaving Porthcawl 9.45 p.m. Fare 2s.6d. NOTE.—Steamer leaves Swansea 7.5 p.m. for Porthcawl.
WEDNESDAY, **JULY 24th**	**GRAND DAY TRIP TO** ## ILFRACOMBE & LUNDY ISLAND LEAVING PORTHCAWL 10.10 a.m. Returning from Lundy 4.30 p.m. Ilfracombe 6.0 p.m. for Porthcawl. Return Fares.—Ilfracombe 5s. Lundy 8s.6d. **SINGLE TRIP TO PENARTH AND CARDIFF.** Leaving Porthcawl 7.45 p.m. Fare 3s. NOTE.—Steamer leaves Cardiff 8.0 a.m., Penarth 8.10 a.m. for Porthcawl.
THURSDAY, **JULY 25th**	## CHEAP EVENING CHANNEL CRUISE LEAVING PORTHCAWL 8.10 p.m. Back about 9.40 p.m. Special Fare 1s. Children under 14 Half-price. **SINGLE TRIP TO SWANSEA** Leaving Porthcawl 9.45 p.m. Fare 2s.6d. NOTE.—Steamer leaves Swansea 7.5 p.m. for Porthcawl.
SUNDAY, **JULY 28th**	**GRAND DAY TRIP TO** ## MINEHEAD and WESTON-SUPER-MARE LEAVING PORTHCAWL 11.15 a.m. Returning from Weston 7.45 p.m. Minehead 9.20 p.m. Return Fares.—Minehead 4s. Weston 5s.6d. **SINGLE TRIP TO SWANSEA** Leaving Porthcawl 10.35 p.m. Fare 2s.6d. NOTE.—Steamer leaves Swansea 10.15 a.m. for Porthcawl.

BREAKFASTS, DINNERS, TEAS, ETC., SERVED ON BOARD AT MODERATE PRICES.
TAKE YOUR TICKETS ON BOARD THE STEAMER.   SPECIAL TERMS FOR PARTIES.
Children under 14 years, Half-price. Dogs, Bicycles, Prams. or Mail Carts (at Owner's risk), 2s. each way.
The Company reserve the right to alter the advertised times or withdraw any of the above Sailings as weather and other circumstances may require.
A reasonable quantity of Luggage (which must be labelled) carried free of charge at passengers' own risk.
The Company cannot convey Motor Cycles or Side Cars.

For further particulars apply to the Agents :—NEWS OFFICE, Station Approach, Porthcawl. Tel. 141.
A. E. SMYTH, South Dock Entrance, Swansea. Tel. 4403.
W. J. GUY, 1, Stuart Street, Cardiff. Tel. 789.
or P. and A. CAMPBELL LTD., Cumberland Basin, Bristol. Tel. 3112.

DATES, LTD., PRINTERS, DOCKS, CARDIFF.

A Porthcawl timetable from 1929.

TELEPHONE No.: BRIGHTON 5478.
TELEGRAMS: "RAVENSWOOD, BRIGHTON."

P. & A. CAMPBELL, Ltd.

STEAMERS:
'BRIGHTON QUEEN'
'WAVERLEY'
'BRIGHTON BELLE'
'BRITANNIA'
'CAMBRIA'

STEAMERS:
'WESTWARD HO'
'GLEN AVON' 'GLEN USK'
'GLEN GOWER'
'RAVENSWOOD'
'DEVONIA'

25, OLD STEINE,
BRIGHTON..................25th May,..................1933.

E. A. C. Smith Esq.,
"Davaar,"
First Avenue,
Farlington,
COSHAM.
Hants.

Dear Sir,

In reply to your letter of the 23rd instant, the name of the present "Brighton Queen" was altered this winter from "Lady Moyra". She is a sister ship to the "Devonia" and has in previous seasons sailed on the Swansea to Ilfracombe route.

Yours faithfully,
per pro.
P. & A. CAMPBELL LTD.

J.B.Mac.D.

This letter, in reply to a passenger's enquiry, confirms the *Lady Moyra*'s change of name, one of a variety of alterations that took place during the winter of 1932-1933. Many of them were of a minor, yet significant nature, such as the signs indicating 'Dining Saloon', 'Bar', etc. appearing in French as well as English: it became apparent that she was to replace the *Devonia* on the continental sailings.

The *Brighton Queen* in dry dock at Avonmouth, 24 March 1933.

The *Devonia*, left, and the *Brighton Queen*, in dry dock. From 1932, the only dry dock in the floating harbour at Bristol was that at the yard of Charles Hill & Son. It was wide enough to accommodate all of the Campbell steamers except the *Devonia* and *Brighton Queen*. They therefore had to make the short journey down the river to Avonmouth, where larger facilities were available. To save on docking dues they were usually dry-docked together.

During the mid-1930s the *Britannia* and *Cambria* underwent extensive refits and alterations, both being fitted with after deckhouses and new funnels. The oval-shaped funnel destined for the *Cambria* is shown at Hill's yard, ready to be hoisted into position.

The *Cambria* and *Britannia* off service in the Cumberland Basin, Bristol, July 1936.

The dining saloon (above) and bar of the *Cambria*, refurbished in the style of the 1930s.

The after saloon of the *Britannia* in the 1930s.

The *Westward Ho*, like her two sister ships, was similarly refurbished, and appeared in 1936 with an after deckhouse. She is seen here off Avonmouth with an uncharacteristically dirty funnel.

The *Ravenswood* at Newport, following the usual procedure for paddle steamers turning in the River Usk on a flood tide. She has run her bow into the mud of the east bank so that the flow of the tide will swing her stern around. She will then back off and drift up river to the landing stage.

Having completed her manoeuvre, the *Ravenswood* discharges her passengers.

The *Glen Avon* in the Avon, 1936.

Aboard the *Westward Ho* in 1937.

The *Cambria* and *Brighton Belle* at Bristol, June 1937. The former Furness Railway steamer *Lady Evelyn*, purchased from W.H. Tucker & Sons in 1922, had been renamed *Brighton Belle* and operated on the South Coast from 1923 to 1936. In 1937 she was transferred to the Bristol Channel and, as an experiment, her hull was painted light grey.

The *Brighton Belle* and *Ravenswood* off Weston, 1937. The grey hull experiment was a dismal failure. Many people said it looked like undercoat and nick-named the *Brighton Belle* 'The Grey Ghost'. More importantly, she was difficult to see in poor visibility. She reverted to her conventional colours in subsequent seasons.

Aboard the *Brighton Belle* in 1938, passing the Monkstone Beacon off Penarth.

The *Britannia* leaving Swansea in 1938.

The *Ravenswood* passing beneath the Clifton Suspension Bridge on Bank Holiday Monday 1 August 1938.

The *Glen Usk*, outward bound off Avonmouth in 1938.

The *Westward Ho* at Hotwells Landing Stage, 1938. She is about to leave for Clevedon, Penarth and Cardiff.

Four

The South Coast between the Wars

The *Brighton Belle* arriving at Brighton in 1923. The White Funnel Fleet did not resume its post-war South Coast sailings until 1923, after the purchase of W.H. Tucker's paddle steamers, *Lady Moyra* and *Lady Evelyn*. The latter was renamed *Brighton Belle* and joined the *Devonia* and *Ravenswood* on the Sussex coast.

Capt. William Bruford (seated in the centre of the front row) with the officers and crew of the *Brighton Belle* in the 1920s.

The *Devonia* at Boulogne in the 1920s.

The *Devonia* coaling at Boulogne. The continental steamers coaled at Boulogne whenever possible, the best quality Scottish steam coal, which the company favoured, being cheaper in France than in the UK. The coal barge, with its crane, has arrived alongside. The coal will be lifted in buckets and emptied into the chutes leading from the deck into the bunkers. It was a dirty operation, necessitating a good washing down of the steamer before the passengers re-embarked for the return journey.

PLEASURE STEAMER'S ADVENTURE

STORMY CRUISE OF THE "RAVENSWOOD"

CAPTAIN'S CARE FOR THE PASSENGERS

"I've met with many a breeze before, But never such a blow," so wrote Tom Hood. That was the experience on Monday of between 400 and 500 passengers on Messrs. P. and A. Campbell's fine pleasure steamer, the "Ravenswood." It was quite an adventure, unpleasant while it lasted, but, in the retrospect, a cherished memory of the splendid sea qualities of a favourite boat, magnificently handled, and of the care, the courtesy, and the kindly concern for the comfort and safety of their passengers exhibited by Captain Weeks and his crew.

The "Ravenswood," which is registered to carry 700 passengers, took up some 300 or 400 at Eastbourne at 2 p.m. Her objective was Folkestone, via Hastings, where some were to be landed and others embarked. Hastings was reached in due course, but, owing to the heavy swell, three distinct attempts had to be made before the "Ravenswood" could get alongside Hastings pier. Undeterred by the prospect of a little "pitching," fresh passengers came aboard so that there was a total of something between 400 and 500 men, women and children. Considering the delay which had occurred, it spoke well for the "Ravenswood" that she got in to Folkestone at 6.15 p.m., only one hour behind the usual time. Several passengers stayed on board; others landed.

A Rough Return.

It was 6.50 when the steamer started on the homeward trip. It was very rough indeed and headway had to be made against wind and tide, which appeared to have entered into a conspiracy of resistance. When Hastings was reached it was found impossible to effect a landing, and it was a case of straight ahead for Eastbourne, which was reached at midnight. Captain Weeks never left the bridge. Meanwhile the "perils of the sea" had begun to tell upon the passengers. There was much sickness and one or two persons fainted. This was the worst stage of the double journey, there being a very heavy swell on the water.

In such a sea and with such a tide, to land at Eastbourne was as much out of question as it was at Hastings and it was suggested that the only alternative would be to go on to Newhaven. This, however, was not in accordance with Captain Weeks's own view. He was too good a seaman to risk, under such conditions and with so many passengers for whose safety he was responsible, the navigation round Beachy Head. He therefore wisely determined to lie outside in the Channel until the turn of the tide should enable him to steam into Eastbourne pier. That plan he carried out. During the period of tension, there was nothing left undone on the part of Captain Weeks, his officers, stewards and men to allay the apprehensions of the passengers and to administer to their relief. Hot tea and coffee were served out with sandwiches, and everything was done to create confidence and make the weary early hours that precede the dawn pass cheerfully and quickly.

The Turn of the Tide.

At 3 a.m. the tide having turned, the Pier authorities were Marconied to know if disembarkation might now be safely made. The reply came in the affirmative and the "Ravenswood" made for the landing stage.

It was all right this time, and by 3.30 a.m. the passengers found themselves once more on terra firma. Before landing they marked their appreciation of the care exercised on their behalf by a "whip round" for the gallant officers and crew of the steamer, the thank-offering amounting to quite a substantial sum.

And what of the Hastings passengers? They had not been forgotten. The railway company had been notified and a special train was in waiting and at 4 a.m. the Hastonians were soon speeding "due east," congratulating themselves on the fact that "All's well that ends well."

Such occurrences as the above are, on the South Coast, very rare. One has to go back ten or 12 years to find a parallel. This was when the "Brighton Queen," on one of her Boulogne trips, did not get into Eastbourne until four o'clock in the morning.

A report from the *Eastbourne Gazette* of a rough trip encountered by the *Ravenswood* in August 1923.

The *Ravenswood* at Boulogne, Sunday 12 August 1925. This is believed to have been one of the last cross-channel trips made by an open-foredeck paddle steamer. The Board of Trade prohibited such vessels from crossing the English Channel from the following year.

The *Waverley* at Boulogne in the 1920s. Although the *Devonia* normally handled the continental traffic, a second cross-channel was considered advisable. The *Ravenswood* was therefore replaced, in 1926, by the *Waverley* (formerly the *Barry*, renamed in 1925).

The officers and crew of the *Waverley* at Eastbourne in the late 1920s. Her master, Capt. Frank Weeks, is seated fourth from the right in the front row. He was, incidentally, the father of Alan Weeks, the former BBC sports commentator.

The *Waverley* at Calais on Easter Sunday, 8 April 1928.

The *Devonia* at Newhaven, 1927. Since beginning regular sailing from the Sussex coast in 1902, the company's base was Newhaven harbour. Apart from those occasions when it was more convenient for the ships to anchor off Brighton, Eastbourne or Hastings, they returned to Newhaven for the night.

The *Waverley* and *Brighton Belle* off service at Newhaven.

Aboard the *Devonia* at anchor in the Solent on Saturday 7 September 1929. She had sailed from Brighton to witness the 10th Annual Schneider Trophy Race for seaplanes. Her passengers saw the race won by an RAF Supermarine S6, giving Great Britain, for the first time, a third successive win.

The *Brighton Belle* at Littlehampton, 1932. Before the war, Littlehampton was a frequent port of call for the smaller steamers but the first post-war sailing was not made until the *Brighton Belle* visited on 25 August 1932. She is seen here on that occasion setting out on her return to Brighton.

The *Westward Ho* leaving Torquay. During 1932 and 1933 the *Westward Ho* was based in South Devon, Plymouth and Torquay being her main ports of call. A wide variety of services was offered, to resorts from Bournemouth to Penzance.

The *Westward Ho* leaving Fowey.

The *Westward Ho* at Mevagissey, 3 August 1933.

A *Westward Ho* timetable for 1933. The South Devon venture was not a success. The number of passengers carried from Plymouth was small and the services called for much unprofitable light running between Plymouth and Torquay. The summer of 1933 was one of excellent weather, but the revenue was little more than that of the poor summer of 1932. The directors decided to cut their losses and the venture was abandoned.

Capt. William Couves (centre of the front row) and the officers of the *Brighton Queen* at Ilfracombe, on the round trip from Bristol to Brighton in 1933. The *Brighton Queen* replaced the *Devonia* on the coast from that year. Between 1923 and 1939, both vessels were commanded by 'Bill' Couves, a Thames pilot who returned to those duties each winter. He was a great character and an excellent seaman who had the reputation of never having taken shelter or turned back, however bad the weather.

The *Brighton Queen* entering Newhaven harbour in 1933.

The *Brighton Queen* leaving the Palace Pier, Brighton, on the return trip to Bristol, October 1933.

The *Glen Gower* arriving at Newhaven from Bristol, 1934. Owing to more stringent Board of Trade regulations, the *Waverley* was refused a No.2 Certificate from the end of 1933. The main effect of this was that she was no longer permitted to cross the English Channel. She was replaced on the South Coast by the *Glen Gower*, which, after certain modifications including the fitting of an extra bulkhead and larger lifeboats, satisfied the new requirements.

The *Glen Gower* arriving in Bournemouth with a good complement of passengers in 1934.

The *Brighton Belle* at Littlehampton in June 1935.

MARCH, 1935.

7 THURSDAY (66—299)

4·47 AM.	South Stack abm.
6·16 ,,	Skerries ,,
8· AM.	Wind light E'ly.
10·15 ,,	Fog set in B.O.T. regulations observed.
1·00 PM.	Picked up Fog signal of Maughold Hd. (hove
4·15 ,,	Off Pt of Ayre. proceeded.
7·00 ,,	Fog cleared.
8·00 ,,	Mull of Galloway abm.

Light E'ly breeze. smooth sea, foggy weather.

J. George
Master.

During March-April 1935 the *Britannia* was re-boilered at Glasgow. Her old boiler had developed a number of cracks and could not be steamed, necessitating her being towed to Scotland. She left Bristol at 18.35 on Tuesday 5 March and at 22.50 on the following night

8 FRIDAY (67—298)

9.26 AM.		Black Hd abm.
11.15 ..		Corsewall Pt ..
12.15 ..		Pladda Lt ..
1.20 ..		Holy Isle ..
2.15 ..		Cumbrae Lt ..
2.35 ..		Stopped & disconnected long towing gear & connected up with short tow ropes.

0.20 ..   Proceeded.

1.53 ..   Skelmorlie Buoy.

2.35 P.M.   Cloch Pt.

4.00 ..   Off Gourock Pier took Pilot on board & proceeded.

4.25 ..   Off Greenock connected up with Tug "Strongbow"

5.25 ..   Moored alongside Elderslie Dockyard at Scotstoun West

Light East to NNE breeze. freshening. hazy weather.

J. S. George.

---

passed Bardsey Island. The rest of her northward journey is detailed in the above extracts from her log book.

A NAVY TO BE PROUD OF

Now we have an opportunity to see this Navy—not merely to look at a photograph or film, or hear a broadcast, but to be actually around and amongst these wasplike destroyers ; to hear the booming of the Royal Salute ; to watch the seaplanes and flying boats ; to be awed by immense lordly battleships, with their lanky threatening guns ; to move like them on the rippling green water ; to see their great bows that cleave the sea, and their powerful screws that whisk a riot of foamy wake behind them ; to feel the spray and taste salt in the air ; with a blue sky over all, blithe and gay with the colours of fluttering bunting, gleaming in the sunshine.

After dark comes the romantic climax. The whole Fleet bursts into the splendour of illuminations, every single light repeated in a thousand mirrorlike ripples, while the sea and the heavens are scoured by searchlights.

This Jubilee year Britons have shown the King that they are emphatically proud of him. Now we have a chance to join him in saying once again, " I am proud of my Navy." And we have the chance to be there.

Come with us aboard the good ship " Britannia," the flagship of the famous fleet of P. & A. Campbell's pleasure steamers.

Completely overhauled and refurnished, the " Britannia " is in practically new condition, an outstanding example of a modern pleasure steamer—in fact, a miniature liner. The photographs show two of her fine public rooms, and there is also a ladies' room and ample deck space.

The ship has wireless. Music on deck and in saloon. There will be plenty of room for everyone, for although the " Britannia " can accommodate over a thousand persons, about 550 will be booked on this day. Splendid unobstructed views from all parts of the decks.

A GRAND SHIP for a GRAND TRIP

We have chartered the smartest ship of her kind. The " Britannia " is just in commission again after thorough refitting and refurnishing.

Length, 235 feet.

Horse Power, 2,400.

Speed, 20 knots.

Photos : (1) Dining Saloon
(2) Lounge
(3) General View

In July 1935 the Silver Jubilee Naval Review was held in Spithead and most of the Campbell steamers were on hand for the occasion. Several ships went south from the Bristol Channel on

the "BRITANNIA"

PROGRAMME

About 160 naval vessels will be present, representing the Mediterranean, Home, and Reserve Fleets.

Tuesday, July 16th. Leave London (Waterloo Station) by special train about 8 a.m. (exact time will be confirmed later) or proceed independently to Southampton from other parts.

Shortly after arrival of the train at Southampton the "Britannia" will depart, passing many of the great and famous passenger ships which dock there, and will proceed to her specially reserved anchorage.

At 2 p.m. the King, in the Royal Yacht "Victoria and Albert," preceded by the Trinity House Yacht "Patricia," and escorted by "H.M.S. Enchantress," with members of the Admiralty on board, proceeds to Spithead.

At 4 p.m. the King inspects the Fleet, and at the end of the review the Fleet Air Arm will fly past.

At 6 p.m. the "Britannia" will leave her anchorage to proceed through the naval lines, and from 10 p.m. to midnight the Fleet will be illuminated and will give a searchlight display.

Arrive Southampton after midnight. Special train departs for London, arriving early morning.

The charge for the "Britannia" cruise will be

FROM LONDON	FROM SOUTHAMPTON
35/-	**25/-**
(Covering rail and steamer trip)	*(Steamer only)*

(For children there will be a reduction of 7s. 6d. in the fare from London. If booking from Southampton only, 2s. 6d. reduction.)

CATERING

Arrangements for booking for luncheon services are explained below with menus, and special attention is drawn to the three services for luncheon. For High Tea or Supper there will be no set times—continuous service from 5 p.m. onwards.

At all times, except during luncheon, a variety of refreshments at attractive prices will be available, or Plain Tea 1s. 6d. There is an excellent bar on board.

The catering can be confidently recommended. The "Britannia" is the principal ship of a fleet that takes a pride in its catering. Cooking is done by electricity.

BOOK EARLY — see addresses on back

MENUS

FOUR COURSE LUNCHEON
3/6

(Three Sittings—see centre notice.)

Salmon or Lobster Mayonnaise
Cold Roast Sirloin Beef
or Cold Corned Silverside Beef
or Cold Pressed Brisket Beef
or Cold Veal and Ham Pie
or York Ham, Ox Tongue.
Potatoes.   Salads.

———

Fruit Salad
or Blackcurrant Tart and Cream
or Raspberry Trifle
or Banana Cream
or Macedoine of Fruit in Jelly

———

Cheddar.   Gorgonzola.

———

N.B.—Book in advance (see centre)

BOOKING FOR MEALS

Meals should be booked in advance at time of taking tickets, to facilitate suitable arrangements.

For Luncheon there will be three services, commencing at 11.30 a.m., 12.30 p.m., and 1.30 p.m. respectively. At time of booking passengers will have the choice of first, second or third service, unless a particular service is already fully booked. The service will be denoted by the colour of the luncheon ticket.

For High Tea or Supper there will be no set time. Advance booking is desirable, however.

HIGH TEA or SUPPER
2/6

(from 5 p.m. onwards till time of landing.)

———

Cold Meat Salad
or Fried Fillets Plaice
or Fried Fillets Sole
or Cold Salmon

———

Bread and Butter
Preserves
Cake

———

N.B.—Book in advance (see centre)

charter. One of them was the *Britannia*, chartered by Frames Tours, who issued the above publicity leaflet.

The *Britannia* at Newhaven, 12 July 1935, shortly after arriving from Bristol for her Naval Review charter.

The *Britannia* and *Brighton Belle* at Newhaven, 12 July 1935.

The *Brighton Queen* (above) and the *Brighton Belle* (below) at the Naval Review, 16 July 1935.

On Monday 22 July 1935 the *Brighton Queen* visited Fecamp – 'The Home of Radio Normandy'. This was the first such trip by a White Funnel steamer. A separate timetable for the journey was produced and a photographer was on hand to record the steamer entering the French harbour.

A special occasion, the maiden voyage of the *Queen Mary*. The Cunard liner left Southampton for New York, on 27 May 1936. She was accompanied through the Solent and Spithead by an armada of excursion vessels and pleasure craft. In this view, taken off the Isle of Wight, she is being escorted by (left to right) the *Britannia*, *Brighton Queen* and *Glen Gower*.

Aboard the *Glen Gower* off the Needles, returning from Brighton to Bristol in 1936. For the round trips to and from Bristol at the beginning and end of each season, the steamers were certificated to carry a limited number of passengers. For those who liked a long coastal voyage, the trip, of about twenty-eight hours duration, was ideal. There was no sleeping accommodation aboard the ships, but the passengers were quite happy to 'turn in' wherever they could find a warm and comfortable spot.

MAY, 1937.

10 MONEDAY (130—235)
● New Moon, 2.18 p.m.

am Mod S.W wind fine
Draught For 6' 8" Aft 6' 6"
10.18 am Left Cardiff
11.4 . Breaksea L.V. abm
12.11 pn Foreland
1.5 am Ilfracombe   Dept 1.6 pm
1.39 Bull Pt
3.2 Hartland Pt abm S W/W
Mod W.E. wind beg Wly swell
5.50 pm Trevose Hd abm
8.13 . Pendeen   var en
8.40 . Longships
8.50 pm Steering engine jammed on
inspection found teeth stripped from
bevelled gear wheel. On chain drum.
9.10 pm Emergency steering gear fixed
proceeded easy speed for Falmouth
for repairs Wireless P.S Waverley
to stand by us in case of necessity
11.20 pm Lizards abm Waverley sighted
Mod East wind & SE swell

Dist run 198 miles
W.H. Bruford
Master

The *Glen Gower*'s journey to the South Coast in May 1937 suffered a delay owing a fault in her steering gear; the above log extracts give the details. The company's head office was notified of her plight and the Managing Director, Mr William Banks, left Bristol at midnight on 10 May by

II TUESDAY (131—234)

am Mod Ely wind S.E. swell
1.15 am Took Falmouth Pilot on board
1.30 · Cast anchor Falmouth
P.S. Waverley came alongside and
we transferred our passengers
9.0 am New gear wheel arrived on
board and was fitted satisfactorily
12.30 pm Weighed anchor & proceeded
2.50 · Eddystone abm
4.35 · Start Point
7.50 · Portland Bill abm
10.25 · St. Catterines abm
12.0 Owers L.V. abm
Light S.W. wind sea mod

Dist run 190 miles
W. H Bruford
, Master

car for Falmouth with a replacement part taken from the *Westward Ho*'s steering engine. The *Glen Gower* eventually arrived at Newhaven at 02.15 on 12 May.

The *Waverley* at Newhaven in 1937.

Aboard the *Glen Gower* sheltering off Yarmouth, Isle of Wight, Monday 3 October 1938. Many of the round trips between Brighton and Bristol were accomplished in fine weather and passed with little incident, but there were exceptions. The *Glen Gower's* return trip in 1938 coincided with severe gales which swept across southern England. She was forced to take shelter off the Isle of Wight and to put into Southampton to stock up on water, coal and provisions, all of which were running low. The trip, which usually took about 28 hours from start to finish, lasted 4 days, 7 hours and 55 minutes!

SOUTHERN ELECTRIC

In conjunction with P. & A. Campbell, Ltd.

COMBINED RAIL AND STEAMER EXCURSIONS

FROM

London
Croydon
ETC.

TO

Isle
OF
Wight

By Fast Electric Trains to Brighton, thence by P. & A. Campbell's Steamer from Palace Pier.

(Weather and circumstances permitting.)

Tickets to be obtained at the Southern Railway Booking Offices, or from Messrs. Thos. Cook & Son, Pickfords Ltd., Dean & Dawson Ltd., and Workers' Travel Association.

For further particulars, etc., apply to the following Agent of P. & A. CAMPBELL, LTD. :—
J. B. MacDOUGALL, 25, Old Steine, Brighton, 1. Telegrams: "RAVENSWOOD," BRIGHTON.
Brighton Telephone: BRIGHTON 5478.

1938 SEASON
June 4th to Oct. 1st inclusive.

A South Coast timetable for 1938.

As the decade drew to its close, the political situation in Europe deteriorated. The 1939 season began under a cloud of uncertainty and ended early in September after the outbreak of the Second World War. As in the previous conflict, all eleven White Funnel steamers were eventually requisitioned by the Admiralty. Most of them began their war service by performing minesweeping duties with the 7th and 8th Flotillas, based at Granton, on the Firth of Forth, and the Tyne respectively. Here, the *Westward Ho* leaves Bristol for minesweeping trials on 25 October 1939.

Wednesday, June 5, 1940 THE DAILY MIRROR Page 3

4,000 Died Rather Than Surrender in CALAIS

One thousand British craft evacuated 335,000 Allied troops from Flanders.

Allied losses in the battle were 30,000 dead, wounded or missing.

The R.A.F. inflicted four-to-one losses on the German Air Force.

335,000 Saved— 30,000 Lost

Heavy losses were inflicted on the enemy on the land, but against this the Allies lost 1,000 guns, all our transport and all our armoured vehicles sent to Flanders.

The French used 500 naval and merchant ships in the evacuation, lost seven destroyers and one supply ship.

Britain previously announced the loss of six destroyers and twenty-four minor war vessels.

THE epic story of 4,000 dauntless men who held Calais to the last, spurning surrender, was told in the House of Commons yesterday.

Of those 4,000 gallant British and French troops only thirty were rescued unwounded. So far as is known, the rest fought grimly to the death.

But they had done their job; a big job. They had stemmed the German drive to Dunkirk and saved the lives of thousands of comrades.

They had written a page—as glorious a page as any yet written—in the history of the Allied struggles in defence of freedom.

Swept Like Scythe

Mr. Churchill told how German units swept like a sharp scythe, aiming at the Allies in the north.

"This armoured stroke almost reached Dunkirk—almost—but not quite," Mr. Churchill said.

"Boulogne and Calais were the scene of desperate fighting. The guards defended Boulogne for a while and were then withdrawn by orders from this country.

"The Rifle Brigade, the 60th Rifles and the Queen Victoria's Rifles—with a battalion of British tanks and a thousand Frenchmen—in all about 4,000 strong—defended Calais to the last

"The British commander was given an hour to surrender. He spurned the offer, and four days of intense fighting passed before a silence reigned over Calais.

"Only thirty unwounded survivors were brought off by the Navy, and we do not know the fate of their comrades. Their sacrifice was not however, in vain

"At least two armoured divisions which otherwise would have been turned against the British Expeditionary Force had to be sent for to overcome them.

Mostly London Men

"They have added another page to the glory of the Light Division, and the time gained enabled the Gravelines water-line to be held by the French troops. Thus it was that the port of Dunkirk was kept open"

The 60th Rifles, Rifle Brigade and the Queen Victoria's Rifles are recruited almost entirely from London men.

Queen Victoria's Rifles (Territorial battalions of the King's Royal Rifle Corps) came into being 137 years ago as the "Duke of Cumberland's Sharpshooters."

No other unit of the Territorial Army, save the H.A.C., possesses a continuous link so far back.

The regiment won the first V.C. ever given to a member of the Territorial Force.

The Rifle Brigade, formed as an experiment in 1800, served under Nelson at sea in the battle of Copenhagen, took part in the Battle of Corunna (a name which has won new significance in this war), and, under Wellington, they fired the first shots at Waterloo.

The 60th Rifles was raised in America in 1755, and for many years bore the title "The Royal Americans."

The Royal Tank Regiment is an offspring of the last war, when in the later stages its units achieved great feats of arms. Its motto is "Fear Naught"

Entente Cordiale . . . British officer hands a pie to a French soldier at a London rail terminus.

Lying on the sea bottom off Dunkirk is the Brighton Belle—pleasure steamer known to thousands. She was hit by an enemy raider. . . . One of twenty-four small vessels lost in the epic evacuation.

This Miracle Saved Our Armies from DUNKIRK

THE Premier told Parliament yesterday of how the Allied Armies had been saved by "a miracle of deliverance" from the colossal disaster of the Battle of Flanders.

A week ago, when he warned the country to expect hard and heavy tidings, he feared only 30,000 men might be re-embarked.

Instead, the thousand ships carried over 335,000 Allied troops out of the jaws of death.

Mr. Churchill opened his speech by saying:—

"From the moment that the French defences at Sedan and on the Meuse were broken at the end of the second week of May, only a rapid retreat to Amiens and the south could have saved the British and French armies who had entered Belgium at the appeal of the Belgian King.

Plan Not Realised

"But this strategical plan was not immediately realised. The French High Command hoped they would be able to close the gap and the armies of the north were under their orders.

"Moreover the retirement of this kind would have involved almost certainly the destruction of the fine Belgian Army of over twenty divisions and the abandonment of the whole of Belgium

"Therefore when the force and scope of the German penetration was realised and when the new French Generalissimo, General Weygand, assumed command in place of General Gamelin, an effort was made by the French and British Armies in Belgium to keep on holding the right hand of the Belgians and to give their own right hand to the newly-created French Army, which was to have advanced across the Somme in great strength to clasp it

Communications Cut

"The German units, however, swept like a sharp scythe aiming at our Armies of the north.

"They consisted of eight or nine armoured divisions each of about 400 armoured vehicles of different kinds.

"This force cut off all communications between us and the main French Army.

"It severed our communications for food and munitions which ran first to Amiens and afterwards to Abbeville and turned its way up the coast

"Behind this armoured and mechanised onslaught came German divisions and lorries, and behind again came plodding the dull brute mass of the German Army, always so ready to be led to the trampling down of any other land which has the liberty and comfort that they have never known in their own.

Writing home the good news . . . two French soldiers in London yesterday—one using the other's back as a table while he "parks" his cake in his mouth.

"This armoured scythe stroke almost reached Dunkirk—almost—but not quite.

"Boulogne and Calais were the scene of desperate fighting—and thus it was that the port of Dunkirk was kept open.

"When it was found impossible for the armies of the north to reopen their communications through Amiens with the main French armies only one test remained.

"It seemed indeed forlorn The Belgian, British and French armies were almost surrounded; their sole line of retreat was through a single port and through its neighbouring beaches.

"They were pressed on every side by heavy attacks, and far outnumbered in the air.

"When a week ago today I asked the House to fix this afternoon as the occasion for a statement, I feared it would be my hard lot to announce the greatest military disaster in our long history.

"I thought, and some good judges agreed with me, that perhaps 20,000 or 30,000 men might be re-embarked, but it certainly seemed that the whole of the French First Army and the whole of the B.E.F. north of the Amiens-Abbeville Gap would be broken up in the open field or else have to capitulate for lack of food and ammunition

"These were the hard and heavy tidings for which I called upon the House and the nation to prepare themselves a week ago.

"The whole root and core of the brave British Army on which we were to build, and are to build the great British armies of the later years of the war seemed about to perish upon the field or be led into ignominious and starving captivity

"That was the prospect a week ago.

"But another blow which might well have proved final was yet to fall upon us."

Mr. Churchill recalled that it was the Allies who rescued Belgium from extinction in the late war

Had not this ruler sought refuge in what has proved to be a fatal neutrality, the French and British armies might well at the very outset have saved not only Belgium, but perhaps even Holland.

"Yet at the last moment," Mr. Churchill added, "when Belgium was already invaded, King Leopold called upon us to come to his aid, and even at the last moment we came.

"His brave and efficient army, nearly half a million strong, was on our Eastern flank and was upon our only line of retreat to the sea.

"Suddenly, without prior consultation, with the least possible notice, without the advice of his Ministers upon his own personal act, he sent a plenipotentiary to the German Command surrendering his army and exposing our whole flank without the means of retreat. (Cries of "Shame")

"Treachery"

"I asked the House a week ago to suspend judgment because the facts were not clear.

"But I do not feel that any reason now exists why we should not form our own opinion upon this pitiful episode. (Cheers and shouts of "Treachery.")

"The surrender of the Belgian Army compelled the British at the shortest notice to cover a flank to the sea more than 300 miles in length, otherwise they would have been cut off and all would have shared the fate to which King Leopold had condemned the finest army his country had ever formed.

"In doing this he closed his flank.

"Contact was lost inevitably between the British and two out of the three corps forming the First French Army who were still further from the coast than we were, and it seemed impossible that any large number of Allied troops could reach the coast.

"The enemy attacked on all sides in great strength. Their main power, the power of their far more numerous Air Force, was thrown into the battle or concentrated on the beaches of Dunkirk.

"The enemy began to fire with cannon on the beaches. They sowed magnetic mines in the channels and seas and sent repeated waves of hostile aircraft, sometimes more than 100 strong, to cast their bombs on the single pier that remained, and on the sand dunes.

"U-boats, one of which was sunk, and motor launches took their toll of the vast traffic, which now began.

"For four or five days an intense struggle raged. All the armoured divisions, or what was left of them, together with great masses of German infantry and artillery hurled themselves upon the ever narrowing and contracting appendix in which the French and British armies fought.

M.P.s Cheer Navy

"Meanwhile the Royal Navy—(loud cheers)—with a whole host of merchant shipping strove every nerve to embark the troops

"Two hundred and twenty light warships and more than 650 other vessels were employed on a difficult coast and under increasing fire.

"It was in conditions such as these that the Army carried on, with little or no rest for day or night on end.

"The ships made trip after trip, always bringing out the men. The numbers brought back are the measure of their courage.

"Hospital ships brought off many thousands of wounded, but were a special target for the Nazi bombs. Nevertheless, the men and women on board never faltered in their duty.

Struggle Was Fierce

"Our Royal Air Force had been engaged in the battle throughout, and it now brought into use part of the main Metropolitan fighter strength and struck at the German fighters and bombers.

"The struggle was protracted and fierce. Suddenly the scene has cleared.

"The crash and thunder has for the moment—and I say for the moment—died away.

"A miracle of deliverance has been achieved by the valour, per-

(Continued on Page 14.)

Eight ships of the fleet took part in the evacuation of Dunkirk. Three of them were lost. The *Brighton Queen*, having made one successful round crossing, was bombed shortly after leaving Dunkirk harbour with 700 troops aboard. She sank quickly with the tragic loss of many lives. The *Devonia* was deliberately beached to act as a breakwater for embarking troops, but repeated air attacks opened up her stern plates and she had to be abandoned. The *Brighton Belle*, returning from her first crossing with about 350 troops, struck a submerged wreck in The Downs, off Deal. She rested on a sandbank and all those on board, including the commander's dog, were rescued by the New Medway Steam Packet's paddle steamer *Medway Queen*, from which vessel the above newspaper photograph was taken.

The Royal Navy's purpose-built minesweepers gradually replaced the hired paddle steamer. Many of them were converted into anti-aircraft ships, but in the latter stages of the war they were relegated to more mundane, yet vital, tasks. The *Westward Ho* was moored in the River Dart for nearly two years where she was employed as an accommodation ship. Without the care and maintenance lavished on sea-going ships, her condition deteriorated rapidly. She is seen here in tow arriving at Bristol from Dartmouth on 19 May 1946. A few months later she was broken up at Cashmore's yard, on the River Usk.

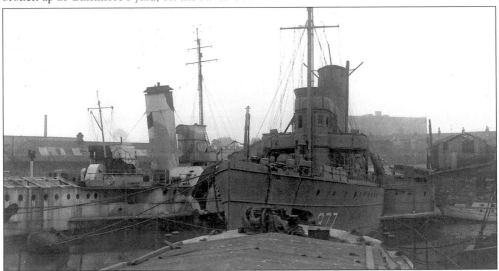

Of the eleven Campbell paddle steamers which went to war, three were lost at Dunkirk, the *Waverley* was sunk during a bombing raid in the North Sea in 1941, the *Glen Avon* sank in a storm off the Normandy coast in 1944 and the *Cambria*, like the *Westward Ho*, was found unfit for reconditioning and ended her days in the breaker's yard. The four surviving steamers were taken in hand at Bristol and prepared for the 1946 season. Two of them, the *Glen Usk* (right) and the *Britannia*, are seen at Bristol in October 1945, awaiting reconditioning for their return to civilian service. Within a year they were once again plying the waters of the Bristol Channel with their decks crowded with passengers, including a new generation destined to discover the pleasures of the paddle steamer.